RELIGION, PHILOSOPHY, AND SCIENCE

RELIGION, PHILOSOPHY, AND SCIENCE

An Introduction to Logical Positivism

by
Burnham P. Beckwith, Ph.D.

PHILOSOPHICAL LIBRARY
NEW YORK

15 East 40th Street, New York 16, N. Y.

Printed in the United States of America

CONTENTS

RELIGION, PHILOSOPHY, AND SCIENCE

"The notion that truths external to the mind may be known by intuition or consciousness, independently of observation and experience, is, I am persuaded, in these times, the great intellectual support of false doctrines and bad institutions. By the aid of this theory, every inveterate belief and every intense feeling, of which the origin is not remembered, is enabled to dispense with the obligation of justifying itself by reason, and is erected into its own all-sufficient voucher and justification."

John Stuart Mill, *Autobiography* (1871), p. 146

"But if theories are merely human contrivances, by which we artificially associate sensible realities, and artificially account by familiar processes for their production, what can we know more than the information which our senses and internal experience reveal? This question is important. It seems also to be misunderstood . . . The wise and . . . the learned . . . propound questions without knowing what will constitute a solution; and investigate nature without knowing when to be satisfied."

Alexander B. Johnson, *A Treatise on Language* (1836)

CHAPTER I. INTRODUCTION

A. *The Subject of this Book*

WHAT IS RELIGION? What is philosophy? What is science? Does each contain different truths? Do they duplicate, supplement, or contradict each other? Is there more than one way to achieve truth? Most educated men are deeply interested in these basic questions, but few can answer them intelligently. In the past 3000 years many conflicting answers have been given by priests, philosophers, and scientists, but nearly all of them are senseless, false, ambiguous, or very incomplete. We believe that the best answers are those given by the positivists. These were first formulated by pioneer or classical positivists—Hume, Bentham, Comte, J. S. Mill, Lewes, etc.—between one and two hundred years ago. However, early positivism was crude and incomplete. Only in recent decades has positivism been properly elaborated into a sophisticated and reasonably complete doctrine by the so-called logical positivists. Unfortunately, they have written almost solely for academic specialists and have used a terminology which makes their writings extremely difficult to read. In this book we shall try to state modern positivist answers to the above questions in words which any intelligent layman can understand.

Logical postivists believe that science contains all truth, that religion and philosophy include only false and nonsensical theories, aside from the few scientific facts and theories they duplicate. They assert that truth (true statements) can be created only by using scientific methods. They claim that no one has ever been able to discover or create any new truth by reasoning religiously or philosophically. If this thesis is correct, it is perhaps the most significant ever formulated.

This thesis is not a new philosophy. It is a vital part of the theory of scientific method. No scientist understands scientific methods unless he perceives why they alone are useful in creating new truths. Many scientists, including some of the most famous, have formulated meaningless hypothese because they do not understand how scientific thinking differs from religious and philosophic thinking. We hope, therefore, that this book will help scientists to become better scientists.

In his famous theory of the three stages of human thought, August Comte (1798-1857) said that in every field of study ideas go through three stages of evolution; (1) the theological, (2) the metaphysical, and (3) the positively scientific. He developed this brilliant theory before Darwin had published his theory of biological evolution and before Marx had announced his theory of social evolution. While Comte's doctrine cannot be applied to all studies, for instance to logic and mathematics, and requires minor qualifications before being applied to some other fields, it is still the best available general theory of intellectual evolution.

Even more important than the claim that there have been three major stages in intellectual evolution is Comte's related argument that theologians and metaphysicians failed to create any true conclusions. It is this thesis of early positivism which we are chiefly interested in restating and elaborating.

Like Comte, we believe that all truth-claims can be divided into three classes and that it is vitally important to understand how these classes differ. But we shall name and define our three classes a little differently. Comte called his classes *theology*, *metaphysics*, and *positive science*. We prefer the names *religion*, *philosophy*, and *science*. We define *religion* as ideas or statements obtained by revelation, or deduced from such statements; *philosophy* as statements believed to be obviously rational or deduced from such statements; and *science* as statements verified by observations. In short, religion is based on revelation, philosophy upon reason, and science upon observation. We shall elaborate these points in separate chapters on religion, philosophy, and science in this order. We shall argue that most religious and philosophic statements are meaningless because they are not based upon observation and therefore cannot be verified by observation, and that all meaningful, i. e., verifiable, statements are scientific hypotheses, errors, or truths.

This theory is probably called logical positivism more often than anything else but it is also called *radical, empiricism, logical empiricism, logical analysis, philosophical analysis, analytic philosophy, general semantics, operational philosophy,* and (by its enemies) *scientism.* Moreover, it is the latest development in empirical theory and is therefore very similar to many other old and new empirical doctrines.

Writers who accept the chief empirical or scientific thesis and reject religion and philosophy have spent too much time criticizing each other and too little time explaining how much they have in common. The content of a theory is far more important than its name. We wish, therefore to emphasize at the outset that many of the conclusions supported in this book are very similar to those found in books advocating scientific humanism, naturalism, pragmatism, free thought, atheism, secularism, rationalism, agnosticism, materialism, realism, ethical culture, semantics, etc. We shall criticize parts of all of these doctrines, as well as parts of older statements of positivism, but we do not intend to deny or minimize the significant fact that they are similar in many ways to our own doctrine. We regard logical positivism as a synthesis of the many sound conclusions arrived at by various schools of empiricists, plus the key new principle of verification developed chiefly by the Viennese group of logical positivists in the 1920's.

The name *positivism* was chosen by Comte, because what we call science was then called positive science, and has been widely used ever since, but it is not an ideal name. It suggests to the laymen that positivistic theories are positive in the sense of certain, whereas positivists stress the fact that no truths are certain or absolute. Moreover, the name *positivism* does not describe or suggest the main idea of the theory to which it is applied.

Some critics who believe that men are more apt to reject positivism if they know what it is have used the word *scientism* to describe it. We agree that this is a more descriptive name and that names should be informative. However, we shall not handicap our statement of positivism by using a new and little known name for it.

Positivism is sometimes called *radical empiricism* to emphasize the fact that it is a thorough-going application of empiricism to all intellectual problems. Since empiricism is the doctrine that *all* knowledge is based upon sense experience or observation, the adjective *radical* is redundant. However, positivists might be called consistent empiricists. *Empiricism* describes the chief thesis of positivism to a student of philosophy much better than *positivism,* but few laymen know what empiricism means. Hence, we prefer the traditional term *positivism.*

Of all the alternatives to the name *positivism, scientific humanism* may be the best. Positivists believe that men should and do use science only to benefit themselves. Moreover, the term *humanism* has more pleasant verbal associations (humanity, humanitarian, etc.) than *positivism* and would therefore be easier to sell. On the other hand, most men who call themselves humanists retain some theological or philosophic dogmas. For instance, most of them praise ethics or morality. Since we wish to argue that all ethical and moral ideas are meaningless, we prefer the less appealing name, *logical positivism.* However, we believe positivism to be one kind of scientific humanism.

A discussion as to the proper name for anything usually prompts someone to remark that the question is "only one of semantics." Many people seem to think that such questions make up the chief part of semantics. This is a gross error. The basic semantic issue is how to distinguish between meaningless and meaningful words and statements, an issue which we shall discuss shortly. Hence, we prefer to call questions concerning names *verbal* rather than *semantic* problems. While answers to verbal questions make up a very small part of modern positivism, answers to basic semantic questions make up a very large part of it. Hence, books on logical positivism and books on semantics have much in common.

Our decision to retain the name *positivism* and our laudatory reference to Comte should not persuade the reader that we are orthodox Comtean positivists or that we honor Comte above all other 19th century advocates of scientific method. Comte was opposed to democratic government, labor unions, votes for women, socialism, compulsory public education, and other progressive things. Jeremy Bentham and John Stuart Mill were, we believe, more able and well-rounded positivitic thinkers than Comte, and Marx developed a much more useful theory of social evolution. On the other hand, Comte was probably the first to state the general theory of positivism, and he ably publicized it and the theory of the three stages of intellectual evolution.

We shall not offer even a brief history of positivism but

we wish to note that a long neglected American writer, Alexander Bryan Johnson (1786-1867), brilliantly anticipated some of the basic theses of the logical positivists in *A Treatise on Language,* first published in 1829 and revised and republished in 1836. For instance, he argued that "language can effect no more than to refer us to phenomena" and that much metaphysics, natural theology, and science is meaningless because it contains words which do not have referents. His book has been recently republished with a criticism by David Rynin. Together they constitute one of the best available introductions to logical positivism.

In this era of partly calculated and partly hysterical anti-communism, any American who studies or endorses an unpopular advanced theory is apt to be called a communist, and this often results in black-listing and denial of employment. Therefore we wish to point out that logical positivism has been repeatedly and bitterly denounced by leading communist writers. Lenin himself devoted an entire book (*Materialism and Empirio-Criticism,* 1908) to an attack upon positivism, and many later communists have written against logical positivism. Such considerations should of course, be ignored by objective thinkers in evaluating logical positivism. Nevertheless, we mention them in order to help students of positivism to protect themselves against their most fanatical critics.

B. *Why Positivism is Important*

If positivism is sound, it is one of the, if not the, most significant theories ever created. When generally accepted, it will change human beliefs and actions more than almost any previous doctrine. The relatively limited and incomplete application of scientific methods to human problems during the past 400 years has already brought about greater changes in human beliefs and conduct than had occurred in the previous 4,000 years. But the changes in the next 100 years will be greater than in the last 400.

It is often said that we live in an age of science. If this is intended to mean that most men in advanced countries have already benefited considerably from scientific research, it is true. But if it is intended to claim that most men now reason scientifically about most of their problems, it is a gross fallacy. With respect to ways of thinking about non-vocational problems, we live, as men always have, in an age of almost universal religious faith. The age of scientific thinking, when most men will think scientifically about most of their personal problems, is still remote though it is coming.

Thus far, only a small minority of university graduates in the more advanced countries have learned to think scientifically about most of their personal problems. Ninety-nine percent of the world's population is still profoundly religious. Even in the United States, over 90 percent of the people still believe in three or more supernatural personal deities, and no laws which it is thought might offend these beings are ever passed.

It is true, of course, that modern experimental science is about 300 years old, and that during these years it has, at first slowly and then ever more rapidly, spread from subject to subject and country to country. Among highly educated men in advanced states, it has gradually replaced religion and philosophy in one field after another—astronomy, physics, chemistry, geology, medicine, etc. And scientists are now mastering the last fields in which religion and philosophy are still strong—biology, psychology, jurisprudence, and the social sciences. The most promising intellectual achievements of the last century have been the widely publicized successes of scientists in these fields, especially those of Darwin, Huxley, Galton, Pavlov, Freud, and Marx. As a result, there is today a small but growing minority of educated men who believe that the scientific method can be applied to all problems in all fields of knowledge. In a few centuries, this minority may become a majority in every country, at least among university graduates, but we are far from this goal. Most scientists are still unwilling to apply scientific methods to personal and social problems. The great Newton believed in witches and daemons, and many modern scientists are religious or philosophic. Few of them have as yet learned to be consistently scientific.

Another reason why the rise of science is important is that theologians and philosophers have no means of agreeing peacefully. That is why mankind has suffered from so many religious wars. It explains in large part why men become so bitter and angry when discussing ideological issues today. Scientists usually agree on basic points of science because they have an agreed method of settling disagreements. Priests disagree because they accept different revelations and there is no way to tell which revelation is best. Philosophers disagree because each of them depends upon "reason" and what is reasonable to one seems unreasonable to the other. As a result, statesmen who are religious or philosophic often use force to achieve results they consider righteous or virtuous. And even when statesmen are purely and intelligently selfish, they persuade most of their followers that their plans are righteous and/or just. Men never fight in order to compel their neighbors to accept scientific principles.

Modern men badly need generally accepted methods of settling disputes over facts. Personal and national interests will always conflict, and will always require local, national, and international police to prevent violence, but disputes as to the best method of solving problems when interests do not seriously conflict can and ought to be settled peacefully by reasoning alone. One class of methods of solving such problems ought to be universally accepted and practiced. One of our chief purposes in writing this book is to help bring this about by demonstrating that scientific methods are the only sound methods of solving factual problems. When these methods are accepted by all men for solving all problems, both the increase of knowledge and the increase of peaceful agreement among men will be greatly aided.

That this purpose is not visionary is suggested both by the fact that Asiatics are eager to learn and apply the scientific methods developed by Europeans, while they wisely reject our religion and philosophy, and by the fact that Occidental thinkers are now striving to apply scientific methods to problems left until recently to theologians and philosophers. We expect no sudden and general acceptance of positivism. But even if it takes another 500 years to achieve this result, it will be a tremendously significant intellectual advance. No intellectual problem is as important as that of what methods should be used to reach true conclusions, and the solution of this problem by the acceptance of scientific methods will be the greatest intellectual achievement in human history.

C. *Why a Simple Statement of Logical Positivism Is Needed*

Although the number of positivists (consistent scientific thinkers) is still very small, even among university graduates, it has increased greatly since the death of Comte. There has been a striking elaboration and spread of positivism during this period, especially since 1920. Modern or logical positivism dates back only some thirty years. It was largely created and publicized by a small group of men at the University of Vienna, the so-called Vienna Circle, in the 1920's. This group was founded and led by M. Schlick and included L. Wittgenstein, F. Waismann, R. Carnap, H.

Hahn, P. Frank, R. von Mises, and others. The new logical positivist movement spread rapidly over Western Europe.

Many learned books and journal articles on logical positivism have been written, but elementary books in English are still very few in number. Indeed, there is only one really elementary book, *Operational Philosophy* (1954) by A. Rapoport, and he professes to be a general semanticist rather than a logical positivist and is much better read in the literature of general semantics than in that of logical positivism. *Modern Science and its Philosophy* (1949) by Philipp Frank, *Positivism* (1951) by Richard von Mises, and *The Rise of Scientific Philosophy* (1951) by Hans Reichenbach are relatively readable. However, these authors are all from Central Europe and seem to be familiar chiefly with German literature. For instance, Reichenbach does not mention Turgot, Condorcet, Saint Simon, Comte, Bentham, James Mill, G. H. Lewes, or John Dewey in his history of positivism. Nevertheless, these three books are excellent, if somewhat Germanic and academic, introductions to logical positivism. Other able but academic introductions to modern positivism are Alfred J. Ayer's brief and lucid *Language, Truth and Logic* (1936) and Arthur Pap's *Elements of Analytic Philosophy* (1949), both of which assume the reader is familiar with the history of philosophy.

We believe that further efforts to popularize logical positivism are much needed. That is why we have chosen the title *Religion, Philosophy and Science* instead of *An Introduction to Logical Positivism.* We have done our best to present this subject simply and clearly, free from technical terms and academic jargon.

While we have written this book chiefly to popularize orthodox logical positivism, we believe that our book contains some significant contributions. Among these are: (1) the claim that a whole theory of semantics can be derived from the principle of verifiability, (2) the theory that logical positivism is based on semantic rather than on logical analysis, (3) a partial synthesis of Comtean and logical positivism, reflected in our title and in the outline of this book, (4) a detailed application of logical positivist theory to religion, (5) the argument that logical positivism is not a philosophy, and (6) the criticism of scientific terms like *law, force, matter*, and *attraction*.

D. *Semantic Analysis*

In developing our major thesis, that truth can be created only by scientific research, we shall rely largely on semantic analysis of religious and philosophic truth-claims. Such analysis reveals that all important religious and philosophic truth-claims are non-sensical and therefore nonsensical, senseless, or meaningless. Moreover, it helps greatly to distinguish between pseudo-science and science.

It has long been recognized that many vocal sounds are meaningless, i.e., cannot be used in sentences, and that meaningful words can be combined in series which look like sentences but are in fact meaningless because they are ungrammatical. However, the use of such sounds and sentences is rare and has not affected materially the growth of human knowledge.

It is also well known that many words and grammatical sentences are ambiguous. They confuse men because they are too meaningful, they have more than one meaningful interpretation. We have all been frequently warned against this all-too-common result.

By contrast, the conclusion that a great many grammatical sentences which seem reasonably clear are in fact quite meaningless is both new and striking. This is the chief conclusion which logical positivists have drawn from semantic analysis.

What we call *semantic analysis* has been called *logical analysis* or *philosophic analysis* by most positivists. That is why they call themselves *logical positivists, analytic phil-*

osophers, philosophical analysts, etc. However, we believe that the analysis which distinguishes logical positivism from other pre-positivist theories about religion and philososophy is radically different from traditional logical or philosophic analysis. Therefore, it seems to be misleading to use the terms *logical analysis* or *philosophical analysis* to describe the analysis carried out by modern positivists. Indeed, logical positivism ought to be renamed *semantic positivism,* but we hesitate to introduce another new name.

Logical analysis determines whether a conclusion is implied by certain premises. Positivists do not often use such analysis to reveal the mistakes of traditional thinkers. Rather they use semantic analysis, which reveals that many traditional conclusions are senseless, regardless of whether they are logical. In order to be true, a theory must be meaningful. Many logical conclusions are meaningless, and every false conclusion can be made logically valid by writing down the necessary premises. Hence, the question of whether a theory is meaningful is far more important than the question of whether it is logical. This is the vital new idea contributed to positivism by the Vienna Circle.

Philosophic analysis is a very vague term. It literally covers all methods of analysis used by philosophers, including logical and semantic analysis. In the past they relied far more on logical than on semantic analysis. Hence, *philosophic analysis* should not be used as a synonym for *semantic analysis.*

Semantic analysis is used to determine whether any given question or answer is meaningful. To explain it, we must first explain what *meaningful* and *meaningless* mean.

1. *Definition of Meaningful*

The verb *mean,* the root of meaningful, is highly ambiguous. A single clear statement may "mean" many different things. It may serve as a password or signal. It may suggest that the speaker is emotional, insane, sick, stupid, etc., or the opposite. It may make the listener or reader feel emotional, insane, sick, stupid, etc., or the opposite. It may cause the hearer or reader to remember something. It may represent or suggest actual events symbolicly. For these various reasons, we often say that events, results, pictures, emotions, musical pieces, verses, gestures, acts, etc., are meaningful. Moreover, *mean* is often used as a synonym for *intend* or *intend to say. Finally we say that a statement is meaningful because it describes or predicts events in a literal or factual way. This is the general sense in which we shall use the word "meaningful" in this book.* However, we wish to define it more specifically.

For us a statement is meaningful if it can be taken literally and can then be understood. *The final test of this is whether those who hear or read it can conceive of and agree upon a method of verifying the statement.* We shall say a word is meaningful if it can be used in a meaningful statement. It follows that only a statement, or a part of it, can be meaningful according to our definition. Acts, events, objects, etc., may cause men to feel or think, but they cannot be meaningful because they are not verbal statements.

Like all definitions, our definition of meaningful is quite arbitrary. There is no *true* or *real* or *correct* definition of any word. The sole justification of any definition is that it is useful. However, since it is hard to change language customs, it is usually wise to define words so as to agree in part with prevailing usage. We believe that our definition of *meaningful* is based upon the commonest use of this term. Therefore, we shall often use it without qualifying it.

Any verbal definition of a word has logical (formal or analytical) implications. For instance, we can infer from the definition of *gold auto* that gold autos are made of a mineral, that they have wheels, that they are a means of travel, etc. Because such inferences are implicit in the definition, they are often said to prove that a verbal definition is formally meaningful. Pure logic and pure mathematics deal only with the methods of discovering and justifying the formal implications of arbitrary verbal definitions of words and numbers respectively.

To say that a word is *formally meaningful* in this sense is quite different from saying that it is *factually meaningful.* This is a vital point long ignored by philosophers and mathematicians. Every word in the dictionary has a verbal definition and this definition has one or more formal meanings or implications, but many words are factually meaningless. To avoid using *meaningful* in two senses, we shall say that a definition or axiom has logical implications instead of saying that it is formally meaningful.

Every grammatical statement has logical implications additional to those implicit in the verbal definitions of the words used. Thus the sentence, "John is red," implies that he is not black. But what a statement implies is not what it means. Every meaningless grammatical statement has one or more logical implications.

Our definition of *meaningful* is well suited to the problem of distinguishing between meaningful and meaningless statements (declarative sentences), but it is not so clearly suited to the problem of deciding whether non-declarative sentences—"Go home," "What a beautiful house!" "Why?" etc.,—are meaningful. However, it can be applied to them indirectly. Imperative and exclamatory sentences are meaningful when they can be converted into meaningful statements. Thus "Go home" is meaningful if "He goes home," is meaningful. A question is meaningful if any meaningful statement answers it. We shall call many questions meaningless because all answers to them are meaningless.

2. *The Principle of Verification*

In order to distinguish between factually meaningful and meaningless statements, modern positivists have developed what they call *the principle of verification, the principle that a statement is meaningful if it is possible to think of and agree upon some method of verifying it by observation.*

This principle does not say that a statement must be verifiable in practice. If one can conceive of some impractical method of verification, a statement is potentially meaningful.

A potentially meaningful statement becomes actually meaningful when two or more persons agree on a method of verification. The larger the number of persons who agree, the more likely it is that the statement will be understood if repeated. When a positivist says a statement is meaningful, he usually believes that a large number of people have agreed, or can agree, upon a method of verifying it, but a statement is meaningful if one other person understands it.

Some positivists assert that verification depends upon percepts or sensations and that therefore a proposition about anything except actual or possible percepts is meaningless. Others recognize that percepts are a reaction to perceived things and say that a statement is senseless if it refers to unperceivable things. The latter principle implies the former since a statement about a perceivable thing can only be verified by percepts, and it is preferable because it does not suggest extreme phenomenalism. Hence, we shall usually speak of perceivable or observable things rather than percepts or sensations.

Marxists have claimed that logical positivism is a form of idealism because some positivists speak of percepts exclusively and ignore the perceived causes of percepts. We hope that our version of the theory of verification will help to make clear that logical positivism is neither a form of idealism nor a form of realism (see pp. 96 and 109 below). In any case, to say that meaningful statements must be verifiable by percepts is quite different from saying that ultimate reality consists of percepts. To a positivist, a percept is a psychological event, not a metaphysical object or substance.

In the principle of verification, the word *verification* refers to empirical verification, to verification by observation. Verbal, logical, or mathematical demonstration or proof is not sufficient. Such demonstrations beg any factual questions at issue. They merely show that certain conclusions are implicit in specific arbitrary assumptions.

Verification by observation cannot be absolute or complete. All scientific truths are probable truths, but they must be more probably true than false.

Some critics of logical positivism have claimed that *verify* is a synonym for *prove absolutely* and that, since scientists cannot completely prove any theory, positivists ought to use the verb *confirm*, or some synonym, instead of the verb *verify*. However, a glance at almost any dictionary will show that *confirm* is listed as a synonym of *verify*, and it is commonly so used, except perhaps by philosophers. Moreover, if the verb *verify* is defined as *to prove absolutely*, it becomes meaningless, for no one has ever proved anything absolutely. Hence, we consider it proper to use *verify* to mean *confirm*, i.e., to prove or demonstrate by observation.

The principle of verification differs radically from the early pragmatist doctrine that a theory is true if it is useful to believe it or to act upon it. It is often useful to believe and/or apply false theories, for instance, the theory that one will become rich if one works hard. This pragmatic test of truth is really a test of what one ought to believe in order to succed, not of what is true.

On the other hand, the principle of verification may be called pragmatic because it implies that a statement is meaningless or unverifiable if it does not matter practically or observably whether it is true or false. All pragmatic results are practical or observable. However, it is the practical results of a statement being true or false, not of its being believed or applied, which determine whether a proposition is true.

Certain critics of logical positivism have claimed that its basic principle, that a statement must be verifiable to be meaningful, is not itself verifiable. This is a very plausible claim, one which seems convincing to many persons, especially those who want to believe that logical positivism is illogical, and few positivists have answered it.

There are three possible answers. In the first place, positivists may claim that the principle of verification is an arbitrary definition, like the statement that a truth is a verified statement. Definitions are not factual truths and do not need to be verified. However, this answer implies that any conclusion based upon the principle of verification is a purely verbal conclusion (a mere logical implication or so-called truth by definition). If positivists want such conclusions to be factual truths, they must answer the above criticism in some other way.

The second answer is that a statement about statements does not apply to itself, and that therefore the principle of vertification does not have to be verified. This is a part of the theory of classes or types developed by Bertrand Russell and Alfred Whitehead in *Principia Mathematica* (1903) before the principle of verification had been stated and attacked. This theory has been widely if not generally accepted by logicians. It seems clear to us that when a man says, "All generalizations are false," he does not intend to reject the generalization he is making.

However, the theory of classes or types merely explains why the principle of verification does not say or imply that it itself must be verified in order to be meaningful. This is enough to answer the charge that the principle of verification implies that it itself is meaningless if it is unverifiable. But logical positivism is based upon the premise that this principle is true as well as meaningful. A principle must be verified to be true. So we turn to the third the best answer to the above criticism of the principle of verification.

This principle can be verified by any careful scientific observer. All he needs to do is to make verifiable and unverifiable statements to a selected group of subjects, define the word, *mean,* to them as we have defined it, and ask them to explain what these statements mean to them. He will find that only the statements for which some method of verification is both conceivable and agreed upon are factually meaningful to his subjects. They may try to explain what some unverifiable statements—like "good men go to heaven"—mean, but they will not agree with each other except verbally, i.e., by restating the sentence with verbal synonyms. In other words, they could not agree on the referents of all the terms used. For instance, referring back to our illustrative sentence, they could not agree as to which specific men are good or on where heaven is located and what it is like. They would, however, be able to agree as to what a meaningful sentence—like "Many women go to beauty parlors"—means. In other words, they could define both *women* and *beauty parlors* by pointing, and they could agree on these definitions.

In this argument we have, of course, assumed the arbitrary positivist definition of *means,* but every discussion of verification must assume some arbitrary definition. And it is surely reasonable that discussions about the principle of verification should assume the definitions made by the logical positivists who created and elaborated this principle. Any theory can be refuted by redefining the terms used.

3. *Meaningful Words*

The principle of verification is applicable only to entire sentences, but we can infer from it several rules concerning the words used in factual statements. *If individual words are to be meaningful, capable of use in meaningful statements, they must help to make statements verifiable.*

In verifiable and therefore meaningful statements, each part of speech aids verification differently. Verification requires observation. Nouns name observable things, adjectives distinguish one thing from another by telling us how they appear different to observors, verbs denote observable actions and changes, adverbs help adjectives and verbs to function, prepositions introduce phrases which function like adjectives and adverbs, etc. These points are worth elaborating. We begin with nouns.

a. Meaningful nouns

To be meaningful, a noun must either (1) designate or denote an agreed and observed referent—thing, event, action, etc.,—or (2) be definable by combining one or more such *basic nouns* with meaningful modifying words, phrases, and clauses. For instance, *auto* is a meaningful basic noun because we can now point to an agreed referent, and *unicorn* is meaningful because it has been defined as a one-horned horse and we can now point both to one-horned things and to horses.

Basic nouns belong to two classes, current and historical. The former can be defined by pointing to their referents now. The latter were thus defined once, but cannot be so defined now because their referent has disappeared. However, current scientific observation can prove that historical basic nouns once had referents because these referents created effects which are still observable and attributable to them or because these referents were observed and reported upon by past observers.

Since words like unicorn are meaningful only when defined by combining a basic noun with one or more meaningful modifiers, we shall call them *composite nouns.* They have no presently observable referents, but their definition must qualify a noun which has such a referent. They include: (1) fictional names, which have never had a referent, and (2) hypothetical names, those used in meaningful but as yet unverified hypotheses to describe hypothetical things, things not yet observed. The things to which composite nouns refer cannot be pointed to but they can be illustrated in pictures because they are defined in empirical or observational terms. If these terms describe events, moving pictures with sound may be needed to illustrate them.

One might say that composite nouns, and the pronouns referring to them, have imaginary referents because it is possible to imagine or conceive them vividly or to draw a graphic image of them. We prefer to say that that is why they can mean the same thing to different people. We shall use the term referent only to refer to the observed referents of basic nouns and pronouns. We shall call the thing to which a composite noun refers an *image.*

Basic nouns are related to their referents as symbols on a map are related to features of the area mapped. For every basic noun there must be a referent, just as for every symbol on a correct map there must be a house, road, river, etc., in the area mapped. If map users could not agree as to whether a certain symbol represents a river, a road, or a house, that symbol would be meaningless, regardless of how many emotions, ideas, or mental images it called up in map-users. A scientific writer acts like a map-maker; he describes the same situation to different men. This requires agreement on the referent of each basic noun or map symbol.

Men can agree on a referent for a basic noun only if they can point to it. All factual ideas are based upon sensation and if there is no thing which can be sensed, there can be no agreement upon referents. However, after a sensible referent for a noun has been agreed upon, the noun can be used meaningfully in cases where it has no referent because it recalls the same idea to those who have observed and agreed upon its referent. On a faulty map a bridge symbol may suggest a bridge where none can be found. Nouns too may imply referents where none can be found, i.e., they can be used in false statements.

It is impossible to verify a statement containing a meaningless noun precisely because no referent for it has been agreed upon. If any noun has an agreed referent, this makes it meaningful because scientists can observe the referent and determine whether meaningful statements about it are true or false.

We are all accustomed to looking up a noun in a dictionary to learn what it means, but a dictionary gives only verbal definitions. As the above analysis shows, nouns with verbal definitions may be meaningless, i.e., they may fail to denote the same referent or image to different persons, even after verbal definition has been agreed upon. The ultimate test of whether a noun is meaningful is not whether it is defined in some dictionary but whether it has been defined by pointing to an agreed referent or image. However, when two nouns have the same referent or image, i.e., are synonymous, a verbal definition of one in terms of the other may help to reveal the referent or image of the former.

All nouns in true affirmative statements must be basic nouns. Otherwise they could not have been verified. But composite nouns may be used in true negative statements like, "He did not find any unicorns."

If a noun is both referentless and imageless, i.e., senseless, it cannot be used as a noun in a true statement. However, it can be used in true statements about itself. One can say that "the word *hell* has four letters or is senseless." In such cases, the meaningless noun is the referent of some other noun, here of "the word." It is not being used as a noun, but as the referent of a noun. The grammarian may call it a noun, but it is not functioning as a noun.

Many words have several verbal definitions, one of which may be scientific, another fictional, and a third meaningless. For instance, the word *fairy* may be defined as a homosexual man, and made clear by pointing, or it may be defined as a beautiful young woman with wings, in which case it is a fictional term, or finally it may be defined as the spirit of a place, in which case it is meaningless. Apologists for meaningless terms often try to justify their use by giving them a scientific definition and then continue to use them meaninglessly. Conversely, scientists often use meaningful scientific terms meaninglessly.

Like symbols on a map, basic nouns may designate events as well as objects. We shall use the word *things* to include both objects and events.

It is sometimes claimed that every object is an event because every object is constantly changing. An iron nail, for instance, is always corroding. But if we apply the word *event* to everything, we make this word meaningless (see p. 26 below). Hence, we prefer to distinguish between objects and events according to how fast they appear to change.

Some basic nouns denote personal feelings or subjective events—*hate, love, idea, sensation.* Since the events they denote are private rather than public, it is impossible to define such nouns ostensively. They can only be indirectly and incompletely defined by pointing to the visible symptoms of the events they designate or by describing the personal events to which one applies them. For these reasons, it is especially difficult to create a scientific terminology for introspective psychology. We believe it is possible, but the terminology used to describe subjective events cannot be nearly as precise as that used to describe objective things and events. That is why some able modern psychologists are behaviorists. It also explains in part why psychology is so undeveloped.

We shall use the nouns *idea, thought, belief,* and their synonyms in spite of the fact that they have subjective events as referents. For us they refer to unwritten and unspoken statements. We believe that when men think they talk to themselves, often, perhaps always, using the same throat muscles involved in talking out loud.

The rule that meaningful nouns can be defined only by pointing to referents implies that most abstract nouns are meaningless. But the term *abstract* is ambiguous. We may try to abstract "qualities" from objects and get a noun like *whiteness,* or we may abstract certain things from a group and get those qualified in a certain way, for instance *whites* (white men). Our rule implies that *whiteness* is a senseless noun (since it has no referent and cannot, like a composite noun, be defined by using nouns which have referents) but that *whites* is meaningful. In other words, the first kind of abstraction is invalid and the second valid.

The use of an abstract noun to describe a quality suggests that the quality is a material or metaphysical entity. This is illustrated by Shakespeare's famous lines about the "quality of mercy" which "droppeth like a gentle dew from heaven." If we speak of merciful people, instead of the quality of mercy, we are not led to believe that mercy is a substance. In a poem this inference is not very harmful but in scientific statements it is.

Meaningless abstract nouns like *whiteness* are very common, especially in academic publications. Even writers on semantic analysis use nonsensical words like *quality, relationship, significance, connotation, meaning, etc.* Such terms seem to be meaningful because they can be verbally defined. Thus we can say a quality is what qualifies, or a relationship is what relates, etc. But such definitions contain no basic noun, and every meaningful non-ostensive definition, i.e., every verbal definition of a composite noun, must contain a basic noun, one which can be defined by pointing.

The use of meaningless abstract nouns in fiction or social conversation is not very harmful, but their use in serious academic publications is often very confusing. Even when a sentence containing such a noun is understood in the same way by different people, it must be transformed into a statement free from such nouns before it can be verified. Observation shows how things appear, act, change, etc. To be verifiable, a statement must state literally how things (not abstractions like qualities and relationships) appear, act, change, etc.

Many meaningless abstract nouns have been formed by turning meaningful adjectives into nouns (*white, whiteness; mortal, mortality;* etc.) Meaningless sentences containing such nouns can usually be made meaningful by changing the nouns back to their adjective form. For instance, the literally meaningless sentence, "Mortality is a human quality," can be changed into, "All humans are mortal." This is one of the chief reasons why sentences which are literally meaningless are still so common and so often understood.

It is easy to define ostensively a basic noun with one referent, but it is often difficult to so define a collective basic noun, one with many referents, because one is usually not able to point to all the referents and there may be widely differing classes of referents.

For these reasons, collective nouns like *animal, vegetable, mineral,* etc., are hard to define by pointing. It may seem sufficient to define them verbally by listing the adjectives which distinguish their referents from other things. But such verbal definitions suggest many purely verbal problems as to classification. Moreover, no verbal definition can be definitive or final. Only an ostensive definition can be definitive and make a collective noun meaningful. If we cannot point to all the referents of a collective noun, we can and must point to a sufficient and properly selected sample of its referents. This sample should include examples belonging to every important subclass of referents denoted by the noun in question. When new items are discovered, they are not referents of a collective noun like *animal* until this has been agreed upon. It is agreement and pointing after discovery, not verbal definitions used before discovery, which determine whether newly discovered living things are animals or plants.

Another basic principle of semantics is that similes and metaphors are always factually misleading and therefore should be carefully avoided in stating or explaining scientific theories. They often make nonsensical words and sentences appear to be meaningful. For instance, one can say that a ghost looks like a man with a sheet over his head or that a vision is like a dream. However, when a noun has a referent and can be defined by pointing it is always misleading to say that it is like something else instead of pointing to the referent or to a picture of it. When a noun has a referent but neither the referent nor a picture of it is available to point to, similes and metaphors may help to describe the referent, but the result is always unsatisfactory. One never knows precisely what a basic noun means until one has observed its referent or a picture of it. In the case of composite nouns one must observe both the referent of the basic noun used to define the fictional noun and also objects qualified as it is said to be qualified. There can be no substitute for such observation in an accurate definition of any meaningful noun.

The nouns *everything* and *nothing* and their synonyms—*universe, reality, the void,* etc.—require special comment. Philosophers have had much to say about them. We can define *everything* by pointing to many things indiscriminately and then adding that it also denotes all other things.

At first glance, *nothing* may seem to have no referents, but, if we divide this word into *no thing*, it becomes as inclusive as *every thing*. However, while *everything* and *nothing* have referents, all statements which contain them as unqualified subjects—"Everything is red"—are meaningless because they fail to discriminate between things and, therefore, cannot be verified. Thus *everything* and *nothing* and their synonyms are often meaningless. They can, of course, be useful when qualified—"everything in room A"—but when so qualified they mean something quite different.

b. Meaningful adjectives, verbs, adverbs and prepositions

We turn now from the subject of meaningful nouns to that of meaningful adjectives. To be meaningful and useful, an adjective must help to distinguish one referent from another. The referents of the phrase *red man* must be observably different from the referents of the phrase *white man*. If a red man does not differ perceptibly from a white man, the statement that a man is red or white cannot be verified and is senseless.

We define an adjective by pointing to some of those things to which it can be properly applied, or by verbally defining it in synonyms which have been ostensively defined. Such definitions are of course arbitrary or conventional. They report an agreement not a discovery or an intuition.

If an adjective is defined by pointing to every or any thing, it is meaningless and useless because it does not distinguish one referent from others. Adjectives like *real, material, ideal, natural, phenomenal,* etc., have often been so defined.

Adjectives are used in two ways. Either they help to designate a referent—as in the phrase, "the sick man"—

or they tell us something else about a referent already designated—as in "John is sick." When used in the first way, they are part of a noun phrase which functions as a basic or composite noun. Hence our comments on such nouns apply also to these phrases.

When a meaningful adjective directly modifies a meaningless noun—as in *bloody nature*—the combination is a meaningless phrase. The result is the same when a meaningless adjective modifies a meaningful noun—as in *infinite thing*.

It should be noted that we have deliberately avoided use of the term *quality* in discussing adjectives. To use this noun implies that qualities are things, perhaps even metaphysical entities. Therefore we have not said that adjectives refer to qualities, or that qualities are the referents of adjectives. We believe that such statements are nonsensical.

We turn next to verbs. Every statement must include at least one noun (or pronoun) and one verb. The noun must have an agreed referent or image and the verb must make some verifiable assertion about this referent or image. The verb may name an action or attach modifiers (adjectives, adjectival phrases, etc.) to its subject. In the latter case, it is performing a purely grammatical function which could be eliminated by changing our rules of grammar. For instance we could agree that "John sick now" should replace "John is sick." Only when we say "John eats" or something similar, is the verb necessary functionally as well as grammatically. In such cases, a meaningful verb names an observable event, so that the statement can be proven true or false by observation.

Use of the verb *exist* has led to much philosophic debate. Philosophers consider that the problem of the "nature" and "meaning" of "existence" is an important and profound philosophic question. In fact it is a psuedo-problem created by the use of a meaningless verb or a noun derived from such a verb. By verbal definition, every referent "exists." Verbs which apply simultaneously to everything are meaningless because they do not distinguish one thing from another. We may be in doubt as to whether a noun has a referent, but if it does, it is pointless to ask whether the referent exists. For instance, instead of asking whether angels exist, we should ask whether the noun *angel* has a referent.

Adverbs are meaningful when they help adjectives or verbs to function. The addition of a meaningful adverb to a sentence must clarify or supplement it. It must add a verifiable claim. In other words, it must tell what to observe to justify its inclusion in the sentence. Thus in the sentence, "it is really true," the adverb *really* is meaningless. The sentence can be verified in the same way whether or not *really* is in it. Of course, the addition of *really* to a sentence like this may reveal the attitude of the speaker, but we have defined *meaningful* so that it does not cover such a case.

Prepositions are meaningful when they are necessary parts of meaningful statements. They usually explain how things and actions are related causally, spatially, and temporally to each other. When they are meaningful and part of a meaningful statement, it is possible to conceive of a method of determining whether the statement is true.

Prepositions often introduce phrases—like "on the way home" or "in his place"—which modify some noun, pronoun, or verb. In such cases, the whole phrase serves as an adjective or adverb and is subject to our comments on adjectives and adverbs. Some prepositions complete or supplement a verb—as in *eat up* or *close out*. Then the verb and the preposition together are subject to our comments on verbs.

Conjunctions connect words, clauses, and sentences. In some cases they add to or change what the sentence means, and thus help to determine what is to be verified. In other cases, they merely make a sentence sound better (as in "I went home and then I had supper"). In such cases they are superfluous and meaningless, but harmless.

Punctuation marks resemble conjunctions. They may be essential and meaningful because they help to state what is to be verified, or they may be unessential and factually superfluous but serve to embellish a sentence.

In summary, every meaningful word in a meaningful statement helps to state a theoretically verifiable fact by adding some detail as to what has been observed. It further describes what must be observed to verify the statement containing it.

4. *Are Our Semantic Rules Too Strict?*

Our semantic rules will seem too strict or narrow to most logical positivists, who accept as meaningful many referentless nouns which we consider senseless. The majority of modern positivists rely upon the theory of verification rather than upon semantic rules concerning nouns, adjectives, etc., to determine whether statements are meaningful. Both methods of analysis yield the same evaluation of religious and philosophic doctrines, but our method rules out many common terms used by scientists which most positivists consider meaningful. We shall, therefore, postpone most of our discussion of this point until we take up scientific terms. However, a few preliminary comments may be helpful.

Those who defend the use by scientists of referentless nouns other than composite nouns often seem to believe that sentences containing these nouns are meaningful because they can be translated or transformed into sentences that meet our criteria. For instance, "redness is attractive" may be transformed into "red things are attractive." If this is true, the scientific terms which we call meaningless are at best superfluous. Hence, our semantic rules do not rule out any necessary terms used by scientists.

Another defense of the use of such referentless nouns by scientists seems to imply that sentences containing them are indirectly verifiable, i.e., that they can be used, either alone or with already verified theories, to deduce conclusions which are directly verifiable because they accord with our narrow semantic rules. We believe that such deduction is impossible, that verifiable conclusions can be validly deduced only from verifiable premises.

5. *Semantics is Important and Neglected*

To some readers, our semantic rules may appear so simple and so obvious that they seem unimportant. However, they have been ignored by many of the ablest modern thinkers. John Dewey once wisely observed that, "to talk about the priority of 'society' to the individual is to indulge in nonsensical metaphysics" (*Human Nature and Conduct*, 1922, p. 59) but he did not explain that if such talk is nonsensical it is solely because the nouns *priority*, *society*, and *the individual* have no referents. Instead he continued to use such nonsensical nouns frequently. For instance, three pages later he introduced a long paragraph with the senseless statement that, "There is doubtless a great mystery as to why any such thing as being conscious should exist at all." His writings contain a great many such statements.

Numerous other examples of senseless statements by brilliant and advanced thinkers might be offered. Indeed, we shall quote such statements throughout this book. At this point we shall note only two more examples in order to suggest how significant and neglected semantic analysis is.

Karl Marx was one of the greatest social scientists of the 19th century and his theories are still tremendously influential. However, some of his most important doctrines—

his labor theory of value, his theory of profit, etc.—are senseless because they include meaningless words like *surplus value.* Thus semantic analysis is most useful in criticizing his doctrines, but it has rarely been used.

The same conclusion applies to the popular theories of another brilliant radical thinker, Sigmund Freud. He resembles Marx in many ways. While he did much to introduce scientific thinking on psychological problems, he never understood how scientific reasoning differs from philosophic reasoning. In particular, he could not distinguish between meaningful and meaningless hypotheses. As a result, some of his principal doctrines are quite senseless. For instance, many key nouns in his theories—like *id, ego,* and *superego*—have no referent or image. Hence, no statement about them can be verifiable and meaningful.

. . . for it is with the mysteries of our religion as with wholesome pills for the sick, which, swallowed whole, have the virtue to cure; but chewed, are for the most part cast up again without effect.

Thomas Hobbes, *Leviathan* (1651), *Chapter xxxii*

Our most holy religion is founded on faith, not on reason; and it is a sure method of exposing it to put it to such a trial as it is by no means fitted to endure. So that upon the whole, we may conclude that the Christian Religion not only was at first attended by miracles, but even at this day cannot be believed by any reasonable person without one.

David Hume, *"Essay on Miracles"* (1779), *last page*

For my part I have ever believed, and do now know that there are witches: they that doubt of these, do not only deny them, but Spirits; and are obliquely and upon consequence a sort not of Infidels, but Atheists.

Sir Thomas Brown, *Religio Medici* (1624), *Chapter I, Sec. xxx*

CHAPTER II. RELIGION

THIS BOOK IS not a history of doctrine. We are interested rather in describing and criticizing the three chief classes of theories now acepted by educated men in advanced countries. Therefore, in discussing religion in this chapter we shall ignore animism, fetichism, magic, and other classes of primitive and ancient religious thought and practice. We shall also ignore the fascinating problem of how or why primitive man first became religious. Instead, we shall give some of the reasons why intelligent modern men are religious and we shall criticize their religious beliefs.

A. Definition of Religion

We use the term *religion* to designate ideas and statements created or formulated by means of religious reasoning. We do not use it to denote religious practices or experiences. Thus our definition excludes both religious ceremonies and mystical experiences.

We define religion as certain ideas and statements because we want to describe, compare, and evaluate religious, philosophic, and scientific truth-claims, not practices or experiences. In other words, our definition of religion, like all definitions, is arbitrary. We prefer it because we can use it to arrive at certain conclusions about methods of reasoning and the theories they yield.

While arbitrary, our definition is fairly consistent with

popular usage. It includes most contemporary theories commonly considered to be religious.

We have defined religious ideas and statements as those obtained and/or supported in a certain way, by revelation, rather than as those which cover certain subjects. For us the idea that the world was created in seven days is a religious idea because it is part of an alleged revelation. We shall also define *philosophy* and *science* by describing the logical methods used to create them rather than by describing the subjects they cover. Thus we shall hold that ideas about the creation or history of the world arrived at by philosophic or scientific reasoning belong to philosophy or science rather than to religion. We base these definitions on the methods of reasoning rather than on the subjects covered because we are primarily interested in explaining and contrasting different methods of reasoning.

We have spoken of religious methods (plural), instead of *the* religious method, of creating truth claims. Similarly we shall speak of philosophic or scientific methods rather than *the* philosophic or scientific method. Methods (plural) can be defined by pointing. *The* religious, philosophic, or scientific method (singular) cannot be so defined.

It is customary to distinguish certain religious doctrines which are common to many or all advanced religious creeds as *natural religion.* These include the theory that a personal god or gods exist, the dogma that men have immortal souls, the doctrine of reward and punishment after death, etc. For convenience, we shall call all other religious ideas *artificial religion* because *artificial* is the opposite of *natural,* not because the ideas are more mistaken. Artificial religion includes those ideas which are a feature of one religious creed only, such as the dogma of the trinity, the idea that there is a god named Allah or Jahweh, etc.

Both natural and artificial religion are supported by revelation. Natural religion has also been supported by philosophic reasoning, and is therefore a part of philosophy as well as of religion. We shall discuss the philosophic defense of natural religion in our chapter on philosophy (pp. 105-09).

We shall virtually ignore religious mysticism because it is a theory held by very few people, probably less than one in a thousand. Moreover, mystics make much less effort to talk sense than do other religious people, and as a result it is more obvious that their ideas are meaningless. Thus Aldous Huxley's key doctrine, that "potential evil is *in* time; potential good isn't," is clearly senseless. We shall concentrate upon less obviously senseless religious doctrines.

Mysticism is based upon the fact that some men occasionally feel remarkably exhilarated. Mystics arbitrarily associate these experiences with religion and try to achieve them more often because they are pleasant and satisfying. Some men have found drugs, ascetic practices, alcohol, and self-hypnotism helpful in achieving "mystic communion with the universe." The great fault of mystics is that they try to describe what is admittedly indescribable, to utter what is unutterable, to conceive what is inconceivable, to explain what is unexplainable, etc. In other words, they try to translate mystic feelings of wellbeing into verbal propositions. The explanation of the cause and result of these feelings is a problem for psychiatrists, not for mystics.

Huxley is an influential proponent of mysticism not because he can explain or prove it, but because he writes fascinating novels in which he pictures his most attractive characters as mystics and his least attractive characters as materialists and positivists. This is illogical, but surprisingly effective propaganda. However, we should not expect a mystic to be logical.

Some religious writers who are not mystics claim that religious beliefs are based upon "moral and spiritual experiences." They even go on to assert or imply that these experiences support religion in the same way that physical experiences supports science. This sounds plausible only because of the vagueness of terms like *moral* and *spiritual* experience. All experience is useful in creating science and all conclusions based upon experience are a part of science. Whether the experience is nonmoral or moral, nonspiritual or spiritual, is irrelevant. In fact, there is no way of distinguishing between spiritual and nonspiritual experience. And if any religious theory were supported by experience, it would become a part of science.

B. Revelation, the Logical Basis of Religion

The most significant fact about modern religion is that it is based on revelation. This clearly distinguishes it from philosophy and science.

Theologians define revelation as the disclosure of previously existing truth to men by some personal god. This disclosure may occur in various ways: (1) as the personal delivery by some god of written documents (the ten commandments), (2) as the discovery by man of buried or hidden writings (the Morman Bible), (3) as inspired writing by a prophet of some god (the Koran), (4) as the spoken word of a god living as a man (the sermons of Christ and Buddha), (5) as the inspired vision of some serious seeker of religious truth (Mary Baker Eddy), (6) as mystical intuition, and in other ways.

Revealed doctrines are thought to be absolutely true. Revelation itself is considered final and complete proof of the doctrines revealed. Revealed truth is absolute, not probable truth. The revealed word of a god cannot be doubted. The human evaluation and interpretation of revealed doctrines may be erroneous, but revelation itself is regarded as infallible by religious persons, and valid deduction from revealed truth therefore yields absolutely certain conclusions.

It is very misleading to contrast *religious faith* with *scientific knowledge*. It is the priests, not the scientists, who claim to have certain knowledge. Scientific truth is merely probable truth, and is closer to faith than to knowledge, as these words are commonly used.

The vast majority of religious revelations accepted today were made to men now dead. A communication from one man to another cannot be a revelation. As Thomas Paine observed, it is hearsay, and should receive no more credit than hearsay evidence receives in court. Very few modern religious believers claim to have received a direct personal revelation, and such claims are rarely believed even by religious persons. It follows that religious faith today is based almost entirely upon hearsay about revelation rather than upon direct revelation.

1. *Recent Revelations*

The process of revelation can be most easily studied in the history of new religious creeds, like Christian Science and Mormonism, for we know more about the form and circumstances of revelation in these recent cases. Joseph Smith, the founder of Mormonism, was inspired in a dream to find and dig up a book written in an unknown language on gold-leaf pages, 7 by 8 inches in size, buried on a hill near Manchester, New York. He reported that with divine aid he had translated this golden book into English as the Book of Mormon. Unfortunately, the original book was reclaimed by its author shortly after it was translated, so it cannot be offered in evidence. Contemporary Mormons must be satisfied with hearsay evidence, but they nevertheless accept the Book of Mormon as divine revelation.

The revelation contained in the book of Mormon has been repeatedly supplemented by additional timely revelations to the head of the Mormon Church. Thus a supplemental revelation in 1852 revealed that Adam, not Jahweh, is both the supreme deity and the father of all men. Another such revelation authorized Brigham Young to endorse polygamy and marry as a second wife an attractive young woman in whom he was then strongly interested.

There have been literally millions of men who, like Joseph Smith, claimed to have found or received important religious revelations, and many such men are alive and believe they are receiving revelations now. A surprising number of these contemporary prophets live in Southern California. Moreover, some of them are dynamic preachers and gifted organizers. We predict therefore that large and powerful new religious groups will develop out of the work of such contemporary teachers.

It is customary for those who base their faith upon older religious revelations to reject or patronize such recent revelations, but there is no reasonable ground for considering them less genuine or authoritative. A revelation can have no other proof than the fact that men accept it, and the Mormon Church has probably grown faster than the Christian Church did in its first century. Moreover, if revelations are to be rated as more or less binding, it would seem plausible to consider the latest the most authoritative. This is the legal rule in interpreting laws and wills. Then too, all revelations are made through men, and men are much better educated today than they were two thousand years ago.

The basic logical weakness of religion is that there is no way to determine which religious revelation is true when they conflict with each other. Each religious group claims vigorously and dogmatically that its own accepted revelations are true and that all others are false, or at least inferior and less important. There is no way in which these conflicting claims can be tested.

2. *The Problem of Choosing Among Revelations*

The problem of choosing among conflicting revelations is faced by the leaders of each religious group as well as by those rare open-minded persons who try to choose intelligently between the revealed dogmas of different sects. Thousands of Christians, for instance, have received religious revelations and have tried to gain acceptance of these revelations by church officials. The Roman Catholic Church in particular, has repeatedly been forced to choose between conflicting revelations to its members. Thus it had to decide which books should be included in the Catholic Bible, and in fact rejected many claims for this honor.

How seriously this influenced Christian doctrine is suggested by the fact that in one of these rejected books, *The Gospel According to the Egyptians,* it was revealed that Jesus came to earth to destroy the work of the female, that the two sexes will in time become one, and that Christians are forbidden to marry.

When the protestants left the Roman Catholic Church, they further limited their bible by arbitrarily excluding fourteen books included in the Catholic Bible. The Armenian, Coptic, Abyssinian, and Greek Orthodox bibles also differ among themselves and from the Protestant and Catholic bibles because the men who edited them selected a different group of available Christian revelations to be included in them.

Christian theologians believe that Christ demonstrated the truth of Christian revelations by means of so-called miracles such as the revival of the dead Lazarus, the turning of wine to water, and the resurrection. (Nevertheless they praise Christ for resisting Satan's devilish suggestions that he prove himself a god by performing miracles). Unfortunately, the divine revelations of other religious founders are also said to be supported by numerous miracles, and there is no way of determining which miracles should be considered genuine or decisive. The vast majority of religious men believe the reports of miracles performed by the founders of their religion and reject other alleged miracles.

It is a remarkable fact that, when men began to doubt alleged miracles, the first to be doubted were contemporary miracles, the only ones for which eye-witness reports were available. This is even more true today. The average American protestant still accepts many old miracles, for which we have only conflicting traditions as evidence, but he refuses to accept the new miracles reported constantly in the press. The attitude of scientists towards scientific evidence is just the opposite. They are relatively sceptical of hearsay and ancient traditions and are much more likely to believe the personal reports of living observors. This suggests that although religious faith in miracles is allegedly based on reliable reports it is actually based on something else.

Any decision to accept one professed revelation or deny another must be purely arbitrary. There is no logical and peaceful method of determining which revelations are true and which false. Therefore, from the beginning of history, religious leaders have frequently resorted to forceful measures—torture, enslavement, crucifiction, burning at the stake, religious crusades, holy wars, etc.—in order to enforce their decision that certain professed revelations should be accepted. During the Inquisition heretics were tortured or killed by millions. Moreover, such measures are still being used. Thus the Nazis murdered 5,000,000 Jews in cold blood, often after long torture, largely because the Jews have never accepted the Christian revelations. More recently, millions of Hindus and Mohammedans were massacred by each other in India because they could not agree as to what religious revelations should be accepted. Even in the relatively enlightened United States, there are innumerable laws, trade union regulations, club rules, trade agreements, etc., which discriminate against religious minorities in order to induce them to accept the revelations approved by the majority. These laws and rules discriminate particularly agaisnt positivists and other atheists. For instance, they are often not permitted to vote, to serve as witnesses in court, to serve as jurors, to serve as elected officials, etc., unless they will publicly renounce their views by venerating a Christian bible and/or by calling on a god to help them tell the truth or perform their duties. Such coercion is likely to continue for a long time because religious men have no non-coercive method of settling disagreements on religion.

C. A Criticism of Religious Doctrines

Religious doctrines may be divided into two classes, those for which some method of proof can be conceived and those for which this cannot be done. The former are meaningful; the latter, meaningless. For instance, the claim that prayer helps business (or anything measurable) is verifiable while the idea that there is a god named Jupiter is unverifiable. All religious doctrines concerning creation, natural history, and human history are verifiable, while those concerning the creation, nature, and history of the so-called supernatural world are unverifiable and meaningless.

Religious thinkers have rarely if ever distinguished between verifiable and unverifiable revealed truth-claims. They consider them both equally true and meaningful. The idea that a truth accepted as revealed can be proven wrong by observation is blasphemous.

1. *Verifiable Doctrines Are False or Superfluous*

Nevertheless, many revealed truth-claims are verifiable or testable. In the last few centuries men have learned how to test an ever-increasing number of these claims by observation or experiment. Most of those tested have been proven false. We now know that our world was not created in seven days some 6,000 years ago, that man was not created, that Adam and Eve never lived, that the earth does not rest on the back of a turtle, that pork and beef are wholesome foods, that prayer does not affect the weather, that women called witches cannot perform wonders, etc. As science grows, we shall learn that many more verifiable religious truth-claims are false.

While most verifiable religious doctrines have been, or will be, proven false, there are a few such doctrines which are largely or roughly true. This is so because revelations contain some statements previously verified by scientific observation. Most bibles include a great deal of history, some of which was based upon elementary scientific observation. They also include many other doctrines based upon naive scientific observation and experiment. However, religious revelation of such truths is superfluous, because they already have been or soon will be stated and proven by scientists.

When verifiable religious doctrines are proven false, apologists for religion often claim that those doctrines are true symbolicly rather than literally. But every symbolic interpretation can be expressed literally by using appropriate terms, and all such interpretations of symbolic statements are, like other statements, either verifiable or unverifiable. Hence, the plea of symbolism cannot invalidate our analysis. It suggests, at the most, that some religious statements are symbolic and must be translated into literal statements before they can be analyzed.

Moreover, those who claim that certain apparently literal religious statements, such as those concerning Noah's ark, are actually symbolic can never agree independently on what such statements mean. A symbolic statement which means something different to every reader is as meaningless as *abracadabra.* A sentence is meaningful only when it means the same to different people.

Because science conflicts more and more with verifiable religious claims, there has been a strong movement to abandon verifiable Christian doctrines. Among Protestants this movement is called modernism, and it has greatly influenced many Americans. Modernists accept the findings of science and have abandoned those traditional religious dogmas which conflict with modern science. Their opponents, called fundamentalists, still cling to these doctrines.

To justify their abandonment of disproven religious revelations, modernists argue that religious problems are entirely different from scientific problems and that therefore science cannot conflict with religion. In other words, they accept only those religious doctrines which cannot be verified and therefore cannot be proven false by scientific research. It is religious modernism that we are chiefly interested in criticizing in this book.

2. *Unverifiable Religious Doctrines are Meaningless*

All religious doctrines for which no method of proof can be conceived are meaningless. This conclusion is an application of the principle of verification and the theory of semantic analysis set forth in the preceding chapter. We shall not redemonstrate these principles here. We shall merely apply them to a few of the most significant unverifiable religious doctrines.

a. The Doctrine That a God or Gods Exist

Probably the most important of all modern religious doctrines is the dogma that a god or gods exist. This amounts to claiming that the word *god* has a referent. However, it is impossible to point to any agreed referent for this term. Some religionists say their god is everywhere, which implies they can point to anything and everything as a referent for the term *god*, but this makes the term all-inclusive and therefore meaningless. To be meaningful, a noun must distinguish one thing from other things. If one can point to nothing as a referent for the term *god,* it is meaningless. If one points to everything, this also makes the term meaningless.

Another approach to the same conclusion is to ask what would be different if the dogma, a god exists, were true or false. If the dogma is unverifiable, nothing would be different as a result of this dogma being true or false. For, if anything were different, this could be observed and used to prove scientifically that a god does or does not exist. In other words, it does not matter practically whether any god exists or not, and, if it did, it would be up to scientists to observe and determine where, when, and how much it does matter.

It is possible, of course, to define *god* verbally, if not ostensively, but a verbal definition does not make a noun meaningful unless it defines a composite noun, in other words, unless it applies meaningful adjectives to a basic noun. Most verbal definitions of *god* use a meaningful basic noun like *person* or *father,* but they apply senseless adjectives—*spiritual, immortal, allpowerful, omniscient,* etc.—to this basic noun. They are senseless because it is impossible to point to any referent they describe. Their use makes the verbal definition senseless. Moreover, no composite noun or noun phrase has a referent. Consequently, even if *god* could be verbally defined as a composite noun, it would be unjustifiable to say that a god exists or that he has done. something.

If the term *god* is verbally defined by applying sensible adjectives—*loving, kind, wise, helpful,* etc.—to a basic noun —*father, person, master,* etc.—the definition is meaningful but it includes living men. There are fathers, persons, masters, etc., who are loving, kind, wise, etc. The only way to distinguish a god from such people is to use some meaningless adjective, like *spiritual,* and this makes the verbal definition senseless. No spiritual being can be sensed.

In more general terms, if the word *god* could be meaningfully defined, meaningful statements about a god would be verifiable, and, if true would belong to science. If such statements are unverifiable, they are senseless because they cannot be tested by sense observations.

The doctrine that a god exists has been brilliantly criticized by Prof. Anthony Quinton of Oxford. In a talk before the Roman Catholic Acquinas Society there he explained that to hear people say that a god exists is like visiting a friend and hearing him ask: "Did you notice our boop when you came through the garden?"

"No, what is it—an animal of some kind?"

"Yes, its a sort of dog; it protects our house."

"I didn't see anything like a dog."

"Oh, you wouldn't see it, it's invisible."

"Well, can you hear it, touch it, smell it?"

"Oh no, its unobservable."

"But I thought your house had been burgled twice this month?"

"Oh, you don't understand what it is to have a boop. It didn't catch the burglars those times, but it knows who they are and its going to punish them sometime. Besides it must have been good for us to be robbed, or he wouldn't have let it happen."

God, concluded Prof. Quinton, is just about as evident as a boop.

The unverifiable doctrine that a god exists will be further criticized in our next chapter (pp. 105-09), where we shall consider some purely philosophic arguments for this dogma.

If the noun *god* is meaningless, the doctrines of those who deny that a god exists or who profess not to know whether a god exists are as nonsensical as those who assert that a god exists. This criticism applies to all agnostics and to some atheists.

It is commonly thought that all atheists deny that any god exists, but this is an error popularized by critics of atheism. Atheism is derived from Greek roots which mean "without theism," and the most able atheists have been careful to explain that they use atheism in this sense. They do not deny that a god exists because they consider the word *god* either extremely vague or senseless.

However, some atheists have assumed that the term god is meaningful and have explicitly denied that any gods exist. This is doubly senseless because both *god* and *exist* are meaningless words.

Theists, have occasionally tried to turn the arguments of such atheists against them by replying that, if it is impossible to prove the existence of a god, it is equally impossible to prove that no god exists. Yet the Christians who argue thus do not hesitate to deny that pagan gods, like Venus and Mercury, exist.

b. Other Unverifiable Religious Doctrines

We have already discussed the religious dogma that certain basic religious truths have been revealed to man by a god or gods. We can now add that this is an unverifiable religious doctrine and therefore meaningless. The words *reveal, revealed,* and *revelation* cannot be defined by pointing to any agreed action or object. It is true of course that the members of a sect or group of sects often agree that certain writings are divine revelations, but agreement on a doctrine is not agreement on a referent. Words like *god* and *reveal* must be defined by pointing before they can be used in meaningful religious doctrines. And the things and events to which a meaningful word or phrase refer must differ observably from those to which it does not apply.

We turn now to a third basic unverifiable religious doctrine, the dogma that every man has an immortal soul which leaves the body at his death. This doctrine is nonsensical because both the adjective *immortal* and the noun *soul* are meaningless. It is impossible to point to anything which is observably immortal or to any referent or image for the noun *soul.* There are many verbal definitions of *immortal* and *soul,* but all of them use meaningless adjectives and nouns. To define *soul* as *spirit, ghost, essence, principle,* etc., is useless because these nouns likewise cannot be defined by pointing or by qualifying nouns so defined. All therefore are equally senseless.

The closely related unverifiable religious doctrine that men live on or again after death is equally meaningless. The verb *live* has been defined by pointing to living plants and animals. To use it to describe what men do after death implicitly rejects this definition. A word may mean more than one thing but both or all of them must be defined by pointing. Those who say men live after they die have never redefined *live* by pointing to men who are living after death. Moreover, it would surely be illogical to define the verb *live* so that it could be applied to dead men. It would be like redefining *black* so that it could apply to white objects as well as to black objects.

Let us consider next the twin dogmas that bad men or their souls go to hell and good men or their souls go to heaven. We shall explain later (Chapt. V) that the adjective *good* and *bad* are meaningless as used here because it is impossible to conceive of any method of determining who is morally good or bad. The nouns *heaven, hell,* and *soul* are equally nonsensical. They have no referents, and those who use these terms have innumerable different images or verbal definitions of them. A meaningful noun has an agreed referent or image.

Some theologians claim that there must be a heaven and hell because good men are not properly rewarded and bad men are not properly punished on earth. Others claim that men are rewarded and punished before death and go on to explain in detail which events have rewarded or punished which men. Thus they say that the Germans were defeated in World War I and II because they were wicked. Still other theologians teach that men are predestined for heaven or hell before they were born and that therefore their own personal conduct has nothing to do with whether they go to heaven or hell.

It is easy for theologians to disagree on such doctrines because these doctrines are unverifiable and meaningless. They are meaningless because words like *good, bad, heaven, hell, predestined,* etc., cannot be defined by pointing or by verbally defining them with meaningful words ostensively defined. As a result, no two hearers can agree on what these words refer to and therefore cannot understand them. They can memorize meaningless verbal definitions, but this does not prove that they understand them. It proves only that they can memorize definitions.

The religious doctrine that the Jews are God's chosen people is also senseless because it is unverifiable. It does not make possible any predictions which can be verified. Therefore it is interpreted by the Rabbis so as to cover all developments. When the Jews prosper, this is said to prove that they are the chosen people, and when they are persecuted this is interpreted in the same way on the ground that suffering improved character. The rabbis, of course, fail to explain that the same arguments can be used to prove that all other races are God's chosen people, but the priests of other religions have used the same illogical arguments to encourage their followers.

Let us consider next the common religious doctrine that miracles have been performed by religious founders or by saints. If these claims could be verified, they would be accepted by scientists regardless of their personal religious creed. Since they are not so accepted, they are probably false or unverifiable.

Critics of religion have often criticized stories about miracles because they believe it is possible to prove that most such stories are fictitious, that witnesses of miracles are credulous and unreliable, that some alleged miracles have been deliberately faked, etc. Modern positivists consider this traditional criticism sound, but they have an important new argument. They point out that the noun *miracle* itself is meaningless because it is neither a basic nor a composite noun.

The noun *miracle* is usually defined verbally as an event contrary to scientific law or outside the natural order and therefore supernatural. But in order to determine whether an observed event is supernatural one must be able to determine what is natural. Scientists know of no method of doing this. When they observe an event which "violates natural laws," they change these laws so as to make them consistent with the new observation. For them, everything observable is natural (non-supernatural), which makes *natural* a meaningless term. Adjectives mean something only when they can be used to distinguish one thing from another. But if *natural* is meaningless, the same is true of *supernatural* and of *miracle*, defined as a supernatural event.

On the other hand, if we define *miracle* by pointing to rare and remarkable events—eclipses, earthquakes, etc.—the word *miracle* becomes meaningful but such miracles cannot be performed by religious leaders and saints.

Some unverifiable religious doctrines are so obviously nonsensical that certain religious thinkers have admitted that what these doctrines mean is inexpressible, unexplainable, and unutterable. Indeed, some theologians have boasted that they believe such doctrines because they are senseless. The influential and often-quoted church father, Tertullian, proclaimed, "I believe because it is absurd" and clarified this by adding that "thought is evil." Such men believe that they will be better rewarded in heaven for believing what is hard to believe than what is easy to believe. Yet they often denounce pagan doctrines as being illogical and absurd. And they have tried repeatedly to express what is inexpressible. A large part of the literature on theology consists of explanations of unexplainable doctrines. A typical example is the following definition of religion by Alfred N. Whitehead:

> Religion is the vision of something which stands beyond, behind, and within, the passing flux of immediate things; something which is real, and yet waiting to be realized; something which is remote possibility, and yet the greatest of present facts; something that gives meaning to all that passes, and yet eludes apprehension; something whose possession is the final good, and yet is beyond all reach; something which is the ultimate ideal, and the hopeless quest. (*Science and the Modern World,* Mentor ed. p. 191).

This masterpiece of obscurantism illustrates both the theory that an unverified religious doctrine "eludes apprehension" and the theory that what cannot be apprehended can be described and explained.

3. *The Popular Interpretation of Meaningless Religious Ideas*

The conclusion that all major religious doctrines are meaningless because no way of verifying them can be conceived raises the question of how men can believe them. Is it possible to believe a statement that is meaningless?

The word *believe* means different things. For instance we may say a man believes a doctrine either if he claims to believe it or if he acts as if he believed it. It is easy to claim to believe a meaningless statement, and men are often rewarded for making such claims, but it is impossible to act as if one believes such a statement, for to act thus one must understand the statement.

Religious teachers are well aware that men would not accept a creed which is entirely senseless. Therefore they have always included in their creeds many meaningful but false doctrines, such as the story of Noah's ark, and some which are both meaningful and true. In addition, they have offered meaningful variations of their basic meaningless doctrines. They justify this by claiming that common men cannot grasp profound religious truths unless they have been explained or interpreted, but in fact they do not interpret. They arbitrarily substitute similar meaningful false statements for meaningless doctrines.

The most common method of "interpretation" is to substitute so-called material for so-called spiritual terms. The meaningless idea that an unobservable, unknowable, all-powerful, omnipresent spirit rules the universe is translated into the meaningful doctrine that a visible (on occasion), powerful, knowable old man located in the sky rules the earth. The nonsensical idea of a spiritual heaven is translated into the idea of a sensible paradise where the streets are paved with visible gold and the solid mansions are peopled with beautiful angels or sensuous houris. In order to reach such a pleasant place, religious men are quite willing to profess to believe some doctrines, such as the Christian doctrine of the trinity, which have never been "interpreted" so as to make them meaningful.

Many words can be defined both meaningfully and meaninglessly. Therefore some religious doctrines can be interpreted either way without changing any word in them. In such cases, theologians can interpret them so as to make them unverifiable when they are distinguishing between religion and science or when arguing that there is no conflict between religion and science, while laymen can interpret them so that they are verifiable and can therefore believe and be guided by them.

D. Wishful Thinking, the Psychological Basis of Natural Religion

We have explained that all religious doctrines are obtained or deduced from inspired verbal revelations. According to theologians, the only way to prove logically that any religious doctrine is true is to show that it is contained in, or can be validly deduced from, a religious revelation. However, there are a great many conflicting revelations to choose from, and many of these revelations contain doctrines which men want to believe. Hence, it is possible for men to choose religious doctrines which please them without repudiating the authoritative deductive method of proving them to be true. In fact, current religious dogmas have been chosen from a very wide variety of inspired alternatives and have been selected because men want to believe them more than they want to believe their alternatives. It is wishful thinking, not revelation, which has largely determined the content of modern religious dogmas, especially those of natural religion.

Most men, of course, never choose between competing revelations. They accept the revelations they have been taught to believe because they want to please their parents and teachers, not because the dogmas themselves state what they want to believe. However, such men do not determine religious dogmas; they merely transmit them from one generation to another. It is the few men who have revelations, choose between competing revelations, or change these revelations by interpreting them who determine religious dogmas, and such men are strongly inclined to believe what they want to believe.

Since different men usually want to believe the same basic religious dogmas, wishful thinking has tended to make all advanced modern religious creeds alike. Buddhism, Hinduism, Mohammedanism, and Christianity all contain certain comforting basic doctrines. These common elements of different religious creeds are called natural religion. We shall now state briefly some of the most significant principles of natural religion and explain why most men want to believe them.

In the first place, most men want to believe that they

have a powerful friend or friends in the sky, who will protect them against enemies and catastrophes and help them to be successful in every enterprise. All children want to be loved and cared for by their parents, and many children never grow up emotionally. Thus many adults want to believe that they have a greater father and/or mother who is invisible but always at hand to help them. Moreover, even the most mature and successful adults occasionally become tired, depressed, sick, fearful or lonely, and then it is very satisfying to feel that one has an invisible friend and protector. And the great majority of men in every age have been poor, ignorant, sick, crippled, old, oppressed, or fearful through most of their lives. Hence, in every age most men have wanted to believe that they have powerful friends in the sky.

Closely related to the doctrine that every man has friends or protectors behind the scenes is the doctrine that these friends will answer prayers. The skeptic may object that an all-wise, all-powerful friend would not have to be notified when we need his help, but men have learned from experience that this friend does not always anticipate what they wish. Hence, nearly all men want to believe both that they have an invisible friend and that, when he does not provide what they want, a personal appeal or prayer to him will be heard and considered. Thus the doctrine that prayer is effective is a basic principle of natural religion.

The vast majority of men keenly desire to be successful—prosperous, well, secure, respected, etc. For thousands of years, therefore, priests of all religious sects have promised that their god or gods would make their worshipers more successful than other men. Most men have been eager to believe such doctrines. Believers have often called themselves by a name which makes clear that they expect to be favored in this world. Thus the Jews called themselves "the chosen people" and many Protestants have referred to themselves as "the elect." And every bible contains claims that believers have been specially favored in the past and promises that they will be specially favored in the future.

Unfortunately, true believers often fail to succeed, while infidels around them visibly prosper. Hence, religious leaders have nearly always taught that true believers who do not prosper on earth will be rewarded in heaven, and religious men have been eager to believe these promises.

Among the members of any sect there are some men who obey the priests much more completely than other members obey them. These more obedient or moral members naturally want to believe that they will be more successful than less obedient members. This is therefore a principle of natural religion. However, less obedient members often prosper more than more obedient members. Consequently, theologians of many sects have promised that the most obedient or moral members will be amply rewarded in heaven if not on earth. Naturally the more obedient or moral members would be eager to believe this promise, and most believers think they are more obedient and moral than other believers.

In particular, almost every failure wants to believe that he has failed because he has been more moral than his competitors and conversely that his successful competitors have used immoral or wicked means to succeed. Nothing can be more gratifying to the average failure than to believe both that he will be amply compensated for his failure on earth and that his successful competitors will be suitably punished in heaven for using immoral methods to best him on earth. Failures are much more numerous than successes, and even men who are apparently successful have failed in some enterprises. Hence, the doctrine that moral conduct will be rewarded, and immoral conduct punished, in heaven is a basic principle of natural religion.

As a result of the age-old evolutionary struggle to survive, nearly all men want to survive. They do not wish to die. Therefore, every great modern religious creed includes a statement that death is unreal, a fiction or a delusion, and that men continue to live after death. This dogma is literally self-contradictory if *live* and *die* are used in their common sense, and it is factually meaningless if these terms are used in any other way. Nevertheless, the dogma seems to please the vast majority of men because they want to believe that they will not die.

We must not exaggerate the effects of belief in this dogma. Men want to believe it and they say they believe it, but they rarely if ever act as if they believe it. In other words, those who profess to believe that men live happily after death are as reluctant to die as other men. Indeed, if religious people did less than other men to avoid death, they would tend to die out. Religious sects survive because religious people do not practise their beliefs about death, about turning the other cheek, about sexual acts, etc.

Another basic doctrine of natural religion which most men ardently want to believe is the dogma that they can avoid the unpleasant consequences of the injuries they have done to others. Injuries to others are normally followed by unpleasant consequences, and as we are human we often injure other persons. Since men never forgive (see p. 193 below), it is very agreeable to believe that there is a superior ruler who can forgive us for these injuries, in other words, free us from their unpleasant results. The belief that such results can be avoided by asking divine forgiveness is, of course, verifiably false, but it will remain popular as long as men want to believe it.

We have now explained in part why most men want to believe that: (1) they have powerful friends or protectors in the sky, (2) their prayers will be answered, (3) they will succeed on earth and/or be rewarded in heaven, (4) they will not die, and (5) their mistakes will be forgiven. These are the chief but not the only principles of natural religion. There is much more that might be said about such principles. However, enough has been said to indicate how strongly wishful thinking has affected men's choice among competing religious revelations and interpretations of them.

It must not be thought that religious leaders satisfy men only by initiating or sanctioning pleasant wishful thinking. In addition to this, they please him aestheticly with church decorations, ritual and music; they provide agreeable social activities; they require days of rest and recreation; they organize charities and hospitals; and do many other useful things. We shall ignore these beneficial activities because they could be performed, and often are performed, by non-religious men. We have described how religious leaders promote wishful thinking because this distinguishes them from scientists, not because it is their sole activity.

E. State Support of Religious Doctrines

We have explained that men originally accept and support certain basic religious doctrines, those which constitute natural religion, because they want to believe them, not merely because they are said to have been revealed by some god. Indeed, religious leaders have often claimed that certain doctrines have been revealed by a god because they knew they would be, or long had been, very popular doctrines.

On the other hand, priests have also based some unpopular doctrines on revelation, for instance the doctrine that men should give 10% of their income to the priests, the doctrine that slaves should obey their masters, the doctrine that subjects should obey their political rulers, etc. Kings and other rulers have long supported priests because the latter have claimed that they can persuade many men to accept such unpopular doctrines.

All political rulers want the same thing. They want their subjects to be obedient and law-abiding, "to render unto Caesar what is Ceasar's." Hence, all popular religious creeds have long included such doctrines, and nearly all political rulers have endorsed and supported the religious creed traditional among their people.

The discerning Machiavelli, who stated explicitly the principles of government which most able statesmen both denounce and apply, claimed that "there never was any remarkable lawgiver . . . who did not resort to divine authority, as otherwise his laws would not have been accepted by the people." He explained that "sagacious lawgivers" recognize that they cannot demonstrate their moral opinions are correct and therefore they resort to divine authority to support their laws.

Most citizens will not obey the laws unless they expect to be rewarded for doing so and punished for not doing so. Since the police cannot watch all men all the time, rulers have nearly always thought it expedient to encourage their subjects to believe that crime not seen and punished by visible earthly police will be seen and punished by invisible heavenly police. This is the chief reason why many rulers not themselves religious, like Frederick the Great, have actively supported religious indoctrination of their subjects.

Some rulers have also believed that the more their subjects think about the next life the less they will worry about bad government in this life. These rulers hope that the promise of "pie in the sky" will make men willing to live on rice, turnips, and potatoes now.

The theory that religious men are more law-abiding than non-religious men is verifiable, but religious believers, and the universities which they dominate, have done little to verify it. The chief reason for this is that the available evidence suggests that the theory is false, at least in advanced countries, and religious men want to believe it is true.

However, whether or not religious men are in fact more

law-abiding, rulers have nearly always believed that they are. They have therefore actively supported universal religious indoctrination and have punished those who attack the accepted religious creed, especially those who deny all creeds. It is true of course that governments have become much more tolerant of religious dissenters in the last few centuries, but many dissenters are still penalized legally, socially, and economically even in the most advanced states. On the whole, political rulers have been powerful and effective supporters of religion in every country for thousands of years.

F. Religious Indoctrination

We have noted that while all religious doctrines are based upon alleged revelations and can be logically proven only by formal deduction from these revelations, they are believed for quite different reasons. Those doctrines which constitute natural religion are originally accepted and continuously believed because men want to believe them. Those which constitute artificial religion are originally accepted by adults because men honor or fear those who teach them and because they are associated with doctrines which they wish to believe. Once accepted, the principles of both natural and artificial religion are taught to all children. Thus religious indoctrination of children is one of the principal, if not the principal, reason why most modern men are religious.

When children are young it is possible to teach them to believe almost anything. They can easily be taught to believe in faery tales, tribal myths, ghost stories, marvelous legends, and religious doctrines. In a word, children are suggestible and credulous. Priests are well aware of this and have usually been eager to control the education of the young. Until very recently, they did control virtually all educations in Europe and America. They have usually opposed the creation of secular public schools because they fear that such schools will turn out non-religious graduates. Moreover, the religious laymen who control state schools in non-communist lands have carefully and thoroughly censored the theories taught in these schools. Thus every American public school student is now required to take a periodic, often daily, public oath pledging allegiance *under God* to the United States. More important is the fact that most American public school teachers are not allowed to teach many scientific theories which conflict with religion, such as the theories of geological, biological and social evolution, of population, of birth control, etc. In many cases there is no explicit written prohibition of such teaching, but teachers who discuss such theories favorably are discharged or promoted less rapidly. Moreover, whether or not public school teachers discuss such anti-religious theories, they are soon discharged if they question or reject religion inside or outside of their classroom. Often, indeed, they are required to claim to be religious before they are employed, and are discharged if they do not become or remain active church members after they have been employed.

The indoctrination of children in religious dogmas is especially effective when it is done by parents who are loved and respected by their children. Otherwise sophisticated adults often cling tenaciously to the religious doctrines they learned as children because they wish to honor their parents, and this is particularly true if they were happy as children. For such persons, even meaningless religious doctrines are pleasant and satisfying because they have become associated with memories of kind parents and pleasant childhood activities. Such adults have been conditioned to be religious.

Even a dog can be conditioned to like a bible. It is only necessary to present him with food and the bible at the same time until he associates them with each other. Christian missionaries in Asia and Africa have found this method of conditioning very effective and use it widely. They provide the natives with food, education, and medical care as well as bibles. Prospective converts thus learn to associate Christian dogmas with services which they need and enjoy.

In spite of the activities of missionaries, the vast majority of Christians have Christian parents. The same is true of Jews, Buddhists, Hindus, Mohammedans, etc. It is even true that most Baptists have Baptist parents. This proves conclusively that religious indoctrination of children is more influential than any other factor in determining what artificial religious dogmas are accepted. If men chose their religious sect as well-informed unbiased adults, they would rarely choose the sect to which their parents belong because there are so many to choose from.

G. *How Religious Indoctrination Affects Non-Religious Ideas*

Religious indoctrination of the young affects not only how adults think about religious problems but how they think about all personal and social problems. Indeed, the latter fact is far more important than the former, for modern men devote little of their time to religious meditation and a great deal to solving personal and social problems. Religious indoctrination is the chief training received by most children in how to think correctly about personal problems, and it helps to determine how they think as adults about all problems. Reading, writing, and elementary arithmetic are as widely taught as religion, but they are tool subjects and do not directly help the child to distinguish between sound and unsound reasoning. Religious training teaches children how to think logically about religious problems, and it is natural for students to assume that, if certain classes of arguments are logical in reasoning about religious problems, they are equally logical in reasoning about other problems. Most teachers are unable or afraid to distinguish between religious and scientific reasoning, and those that do distinguish are unable to explain why religious reasoning should be confined to religious problems and how to distinguish between religious and non-religious problems. Many theologians, indeed, hold that all, or nearly all, important problems of conduct are religious problems, and few teachers can and do refute them.

1. *It Makes Men Dogmatic, Arrogant, and Intolerant*

Perhaps the most unfortunate result of religious indoctrination is that it makes men authoritative and dogmatic. It teaches them to rely upon traditional doctrines and prejudices rather than upon their own observation and judgment or upon that of qualified scientists. This discourages new scientific research on problems of personal and social conduct.

Teachers of religion have often taught that men should believe what is absurd or unintelligible simply because it is accepted by religious authorities. Tertullian said, "Thought is evil" and Tolstoy, a devout Christian, warned that "He who has learned to reason finds it hard to believe." As a result, many men come to believe that it is wrong to think independently about any problems. With the rise of scientific research, independent thinking has become more general, but this has caused the priests to warn against such thinking on religious matters more strongly than ever. It is increasingly difficult for men to accept authoritative pronouncements on some subjects but not on others.

To be authoritative and dogmatic in the absence of convincing scientific evidence, one must be intellectually arrogant. Religious indoctrination makes men intellectually arrogant. Students of religion are taught to believe that their own sectarian dogmas are absolutely true and that conflicting dogmas of other sects are absolutely false. Since these competing dogmas are likewise based upon professed revelation, and there is no way to evaluate revelations, the true believer must be conceited enough to assert that his dogmas and revelations are true and others false even though he cannot possibly prove this.

Paradoxically, it is the scientists, who can offer objective evidence that their beliefs are true, who are intellectually humble. They often emphasize that the truths of science are incomplete, imperfect, relative and subject to continuing correction. Perhaps that is one reason why educated Asians and Africans are much more eager to accept European science than European religion.

Religious indoctrination also makes men intolerant. This well-known result is important, but it has been explained and illustrated so often that it requires little elaboration here. Wars due in part to the fact that religious men are intolerant have repeatedly devastated most countries in Europe and Asia. It was only a few hundred years ago that Catholics and Protestants were burning each other at the stake throughout Europe. And it is less than two centuries since Jews and Catholics were first allowed to vote and serve as public officials in protestant countries. Moreover, religious minorities are still discriminated against in almost every country. At least 10,000,000 Jews, Hindus, Mohammedans, Armenians, etc., have been murdered by their religious rivals since 1900.

Men who have been taught to be religiously intolerant tend to be politically intolerant. Religious indoctrination is partly, perhaps largely, responsible for the fact that voters and politicians are so often arrogant and intolerant. In particular, the persecution of political radicals in every country and age is partly due to religious indoctrination. The first democrats, the American abolitionists, the pioneer trade union organizers, the anarchists, the socialists, the communists have all been persecuted by men made intolerant by religious indoctrination.

The fact that dogmatic indoctrination can make even non-religious men dogmatic, arrogant, and intolerant is illustrated most clearly today by the behavior of Russian Communists. Although these men reject religion, they have been powerfully influenced by a thousand years of Christian indoctrination. Stalin was educated in a religious seminary. Pre-revolutionary Russia was one of the most religious and backward nations in Europe. Indeed, the Russian people are still deeply religious and hence accustomed to authoritative guidance. It is natural, therefore, that the Communists should have known and applied to economic and political problems the same methods of reasoning, government, party organization, propaganda, discipline, censorship, etc., which the Russian Catholic Church had long practised.

It is a remarkable fact that the Roman Catholic Church, the closest Western equivalent to the Russian Orthodox Church, markedly resembles the Russian Communist movement. Each has its inspired founders, its written revelation, its creed, its infallible pope, its bulls, its self-perpetuating undemocratic ruling group which selects the new pope, its index of disapproved books, its censors of art and literature, its immense public parades and assemblies, its hymns, its propagandistic art, its vows of loyalty, its dedicated clergy, its sacraments, its martyrs, its heretics, its inquisition, its agencies of international propaganda, its devotees, its plans for world domination, its ambassadors, its missionaries, its anathemas, its ascetic rules for devotees, etc.

No wonder communism is often called a religion! Nor is it surprising that communists are far more numerous in catholic than in protestant lands, or that communist apostates so often become devout catholics, even in protestant countries. Intolerant dogmatists of the left and the right have much in common.

2. *It Makes Men Wishful and Credulous Thinkers*

Religious indoctrination encourages men to rely upon wishful thinking rather than constructive action in solving practical problems. If it is proper to believe that we have an invisible friend or that we will never die because this satisfies us emotionally, is it not equally proper to believe that we will win the next war or the next election for the same reason? Most serious, of course, is the fact that religious indoctrination makes some men believe that the mere wishing is enough, especially when it becomes explicit formal prayer. For thousands of years priests have taught that prayer will bring rain or sunshine, heal the sick and lame, win wars, and prevent natural catastrophes.

It is impossible to believe that wishful thinking will help to achieve desired results without doing less in other ways to achieve these results. Every moment devoted to prayer is one moment less devoted to constructive problem-solving thought or action. And faith in prayer has often caused men to rely entirely on prayer to solve their problems. Conversely, every advance in applied science helps men to solve their problems and makes prayer less urgent and less frequent.

Religious indoctrination makes men credulous on non-religious subjects. Men who have been taught that angels, devils, and cherubim exist, that souls migrate from insects to men, or that miracles have been seen find it relatively easy to believe in flying saucers, sea monsters, dragons, witches, ghosts, palmistry, astrology, water divining, and numerology.

3. *It slows the Growth of Scientific Research*

Moreover, religious indoctrination delays scientific progress. We have explained why such teaching makes men authoritative, arrogant, intolerant, wishful-thinking, and credulous in reasoning about non-religious as well as religious problems. Such men are less capable of advancing science than their opposites. Also, religious indoctrination has slowed the growth of scientific thinking and research by other means.

First, by providing answers to many scientific questions—in the story of creation, of the flood, of human history, etc.—it has made men think they know the answer to these questions and has thus made scientific research seem unnecessary. Moreover, by persecuting pioneer scientists who questioned religious answers to these problems, religious leaders made scientific reasoning dangerous.

Thirdly, theologians have always claimed that many personal problems belong to religion and not to science, and they have proclaimed moral rules of conduct which they assert cannot and should not be challenged by scientists. This theory is still a serious obstacle to scientific research in the life and social sciences.

Fourthly, education in science is severely restricted both in church schools and in the public schools which religious voters control. Scientific theories which contradict religious doctrines are usually ignored or misrepresented, and the amount of time devoted to other scientific theories is far less than it should be in order to promote social progress.

Finally, theologians have applied their dogmatic moral rules to scientific research and have forbidden many promising research methods and projects. For instance, the use of human cadavers for anatomical research and teaching was blocked for a thousand years in Europe. Vivisection, invaluable in medical research, is opposed today by many people on religious grounds. Moreover, priests disprove of tests to determine whether theories of human eugenics are sound, whether new medicines will work if this involves risks, how children would behave if raised without human companions, etc. They have even got famous psychologists fired for taking nude photos of students for research purposes or for asking students to fill in questionnaires containing queries on sexual behavior.

4. *It Delays Social Reforms*

Religious indoctrination blocks or delays social reforms. As we have explained, religious thinkers rely dogmatically upon authorities. The majority of the most honored religious authorities lived a very long time ago. They were therefore unfamiliar with most of the social problems we face today. Moreover, because they were especially interested in problems of "the next world," they devoted little thought to the social problems of their own time, such as war and slavery. In fact, they often endorsed existing social and political customs in order to avoid persecution and/or in order to concentrate upon "spiritual" things. For these and other reasons, religious indoctrination has made religious people hostile to needed social reforms. The great revolutionists and reformers of the past 200 years have for the most part rejected orthodox religion, while the official heads of religious groups have opposed nearly all successful reforms and revolutions. We could cite many instances of this, but a few must suffice. One of the greatest reforms in the history of the United States was the abolition of slavery, an institution which was supported by virtually all Christian ministers in the slave states until its end. In the northern states, a few ministers condemned slavery in the South, but it is always easy, and often pleasant, to criticize one's neighbors.

Another great reform of the last century has been the rise of birth control, which is largely responsible for the fact that real wages are today so much higher in occidental than in oriental lands. This reform has been opposed by the vast majority of priests. Now that the reform has been largely achieved in the most advanced states, some Protestant ministers openly support it. It is significant that these ministers began to practice birth control long before they were willing to advocate it. Even today, birth control is far more widely practised than preached by Protestant ministers.

A third great reform of the past century has been the emancipation of women from legal, social, and economic discrimination. This reform is not yet complete or universal, but it has gone far. Christian ministers not only failed to lead this reform but on the whole opposed it. They still fight against the last steps in this reform, especially in Catholic countries, where women are far from being legally free.

Perhaps the greatest reform now being debated in advanced countries is democratic socialism. While there are some Protestant ministers who have supported this reform, the great bulk of the clergy has consistently opposed it even in countries like England and Sweden where socialist governments have repeatedly been elected. The Pope has explicitly condemned socialism, as well as artificial birth control, as immoral. Thus it is clear that religious thinkers, who profess to be skillful in judging moral issues, are the last to support the great reforms which benefit the community. Religious teachers emphasize faith and resignation, not social research and political reform.

H. Causes Which Have Made Modern Men less Religious

We have explained why for thousands of years nearly all men were religious. In the last two centuries, however, a small but steadily growing number of men have not only rejected all religious theories but have actively published and taught their anti-religious views. Moreover, a much older and larger group of critics has attacked individual religious dogmas such as that of the virgin birth of Christ. The people of the most advanced western countries have been becoming less and less religious for at least 400 years. We shall now discuss briefly the reasons for this tremendously significant change.

1. *The Rise of Science*

The chief cause is probably the steady and unparalleled growth of pure and applied science. This in turn is a result of the creation and steady elaboration of the theory of scientific reasoning and research.

During the past 400 years, scientists have solved one human problem after another. Before scientists created the theory of evolution, men had no plausible alternative to religious stories about the history of men and the world. Until modern scientists learned how to cure the sick, men naturally wanted to believe that prayer and medicine men could do so. With the growth of medical science, men learn to rely more and more on professional scientific advice and treatment and less and less on wishful religious thinking.

Many other illustrations of the way in which scientific research has made the people of advanced countries more secure, more prosperous, more confident, and more self-reliant might be given. And it is precisely in technologically advanced states that men have become least religious.

2. *The Growth of Education*

Another major cause of the decline in religious faith in advanced countries during recent centuries has been the rapid increase in the number of literate and educated persons. Three centuries ago less than 10% of Europeans could read and write. Today 90% are literate. And the number of university graduates has increased a thousandfold in the same period.

The effects of education upon religious ideas can be shown most easily and clearly by comparing the professed religious opinions of university students and graduates with those of less educated men. The data is still scant and very incompletely reported (because religious men, who control most research, suspect that religious people are less educated than atheists), but the findings already published are revealing.

The first and the ablest scientist to use opinion polls to determine how education affects religious opinion was James H. Leuba, a psychologist. In 1912 he polled students in several classes in ten American colleges. He found that only 56% of the men and 83% of the women believed in a personal god who answers prayer.[1]

In 1933 Leuba polled over 90% of the students in two colleges. The results are shown in Table I.

TABLE I
BELIEVERS IN A PERSONAL GOD

	COLLEGE A	COLLEGE B
Freshman	34%	20%
Sophomore	37%	14%
Juniors	30%	6%
Seniors	20%	5%

It is significant that the percentage of believers among

[1] Our report on Leuba's work is based on his book, *The Reformation of the Churches,* Beacon Press, Boston, 1950.

freshmen was far below most estimates for non-college men, and that this percentage dropped with every year of additional education.

In 1914 Leuba asked all students in College A if they believed in personal immortality. In 1933 he asked the same question of all students in both college A and college B. In each case he received answers from over 90% of the students. The results are shown in Table II.

TABLE II
EFFECT OF EDUCATION ON BELIEF IN IMMORTALITY

	College A—1914 & 1933						College B—1933		
	% Believe		% Doubt		% Disbelieve		% Believe	% Doubt	% Disbelieve
	1914	1933	1914	1933	1914	1933			
FRESHMAN	80	42	5	25	15	33	29	28	44
SOPHOMORES	76	50	5	20	19	30	20	36	44
JUNIORS	60	37	8	26	32	37	14	23	63
SENIORS	70	27	6	26	24	47	5	27	68

Here again we see that college students become less religious with every additional year of higher education. Moreover, they were much less religious in 1933 than in 1914.

Leuba also polled scientists on their religious opinions in 1914 and 1933. He obtained his names from Cattell's well-known directory, *American Men of Science,* and from the membership lists of learned societies. The most eminent scientists in the directory are starred, and Leuba prepared lists of eminent scientists in other fields. Thus he was able to compare the religious opinions of the leading scientists in each group with those of less eminent men. Sixty per cent of the scientists covered were college professors. Questionnaires were not sent to scientists teaching in Catholic schools, but these were few in number. The results are tabulated in Table III.

TABLE III
COMPARISON OF RELIGIOUS OPINIONS
OF GREATER AND LESSER SCIENTISTS,
1914 and 1933

		Percent Believing in Personal God		Percent Believing in Immortality	
	Year	Lesser	Greater	Lesser	Greater
Inorganic Scientists	1914	50	35	57	40
	1933	43	17	46	20
Life Scientists	1914	39	17	45	25
	1933	31	12	32	15
Sociologists	1914	29	19	52	27
	1933	30	13	31	10
Psychologists	1914	32	13	27	9
	1933	13	12	12	2
Historians	1914	63	33	68	25

Table III shows: (1) that the percentage of religious scientists declined sharply from 1914 to 1933, and (2) that in both years the greater scientists were far less religious than the lesser scientists.

In 1926 a survey of the religious opinions of Syracuse University students was made by D. Katz and F. Allport. They found that 39% of the students believed in a personal god when they entered Syracuse, but only 21% so believed one to four years later. Many of them shifted to belief in an impersonal spiritual being, not to agnosticism or atheism.

In 1946 a survey of the religious opinions of 414 Harvard and 86 Radcliffe undergraduates was made by G. W. Allport, J. M. Gillespie, and Jacqueline Young. They found that only 47% of these students believed in a personal god, that women were much more religious than men (59% as compared with 45% for men), and that the war veterans (42%) were much less religious than the younger and less sophisticated non-veterans (52%). Only 25% indicated that they believed in "personal immortality." There are other findings in this study which support the authors' conclusion that "only about one-quarter of the students are orthodox in their [religious] position."

This study also included questions concerning the religious opinions of the parents of these students and their early religious indoctrination. The answers disclose that half of all students, but none of the women, had abandoned the traditional religious opinions of their parents and become either markedly less religious or non-religious. About 25% of all students with religious parents had become completely irreligious, according to these authors, and we would estimate this last figure at 50%. We think that those who indicated they believe neither in a personal god nor in personal immortality were nearly all irreligious. Moreover, over half of all students noted that they approved of John Dewey's assertion that religion "should have nothing to do with supernatural notions."

Allport and his associates were apparently disappointed with their findings. Some of their questions and conclusions were clearly biased in favor of religion. For instance, they asserted that university graduates become more religious as they become older, although their own study showed that war veterans were much less religious than younger students. They cited no statistics to support this assertion and we know of none.

If Allport and his associates had desired to do so, they could easily have determined whether the more religious students made as good grades and as high I.Q. scores as the less religious students. Leuba's brilliant pioneer studies had clearly suggested that more able students and graduates are much less religious than other students. Unfortunately, Allport and associates either did not investigate this vital question or failed to publish their findings.

In 1953 a survey of religious attitudes was made by a commercial opinion research firm for the *Catholic Digest.* According to this report, the number of atheists among the general American population over 18 is only a little over 1%, but the number among college graduates is 4%, or 300% more than for non-college graduates. It was also reported that only 12% of the general population regard Christ as a man rather than a god while 27% of college graduates so regard him.

Since all other surveys, including several not quoted above, report a much higher percentage of non-believers, this Catholic survey was probably biased. However, there are explanations which may account for some of the Catholic results. Earlier studies covered students at superior northern non-denominational colleges and alumni who were scientists. Graduates of inferior northern schools, southern schools, and Catholic schools are probably much more religious, and those who do not secure graduate degrees are probably much more religious than those who do. Nevertheless, we predict that future studies will discredit the Catholic survey finding.

We also confidently predict that further studies will support the following conclusions:

(1) Every additional year of education above the 12th perhaps the 8th, grade makes men less religious.

(2) Among men with the same education, those who make the highest grades and/or I.Q. scores are the least religious.

(3) College graduates are far less religious than their parents.

3. *Minor Causes*

We have discussed the chief causes of the long decline in the number of religious persons and the number of religious dogmas they accept, namely the rapid growth of science and the rapid increase in the class of educated men. We turn now to some minor causes.

A number of writers have claimed that men become less religious when they move from the farm to the town or city, and we agree. This change is due in part to the fact that urban people become better educated than farmers. It is also due in part to the fact that farmers are closer to and more dependent upon natural phenomena which men cannot understand and control—the germination of seeds, the birth of animals, floods, drouths, tornadoes, hail storms, etc. Men resort to prayer chiefly when they know no better means of controlling events. By comparison, town dwellers are relatively free from the effects of natural disasters and they invent and build tools and machines which make them feel more confident and independent.

Most city dwellers were born on a farm or are the children or grandchildren of men raised on the farm. It takes several generations for men to adjust at all fully to a new environment. Moreover, the shift from farm to city will continue until less than 2% of our people work on the farm. Finally, the radio, the telephone, the television, the movies, and the growth of scientific farming will make the remaining farmers more and more like city people in religious opinion.

Comte said that theology and militarism, science and industrialism, go together. This is a stimulating theory but it is only a corollary of the more basic principle that everything which makes men feel insecure and dependent on uncontrollable events make them more religious. Wars often result from militarism, and vice versa, and wars make men feel insecure and therefore more religious. When wars have been eliminated by a world state, they will no longer make men religious.

Another minor cause which has helped to make liberal religious doctrines and positivism more popular in the last few centuries is that critics of conservative religious creeds have been much more free to express themselves. There may have been silent atheists before 1700 but we know of no outspoken ones. The first men in Christian Europe who dared to attack theism openly and directly were the more advanced precursors of the French Revolution, men like d'Holbach, Volney, and Meslier. Fifty years later, the first outspoken English atheists were jailed or fined for their anti-religious publications. Jeremy Bentham did not dare publish his attacks upon religion under his own name. However, critics of religion have felt more and more free to publish their arguments since then. The number of their publications has increased rapidly and they have influenced a steadily growing group of readers. Today it is easier than ever before for young people to find a reasoned statement of the arguments against religion, and this has helped to make them less religious. However, even today few young people read such anti-religious statements before they formally join a church.

We have now explained both the age-old reasons and causes which have made most men religious and the new and increasingly effective reasons and causes which have been making modern men less and less religious for several centuries. Since the old causes are becoming weaker while the new factors are becoming steadily stronger, and will continue to do so indefinitely, men will become less and less religious for a very long time. It will be possible to verify this prediction by suitable public opinion polls. We are confident that such polls will become more accurate and more frequent and that they will support our predictions.

"If we take in our hand any volume; of divinity, or school metaphysics, for instance; let us ask, Does it contain any abstract reasoning concerning quantity or number? No. Does it contain any experimental reasoning concerning matter of fact and existence? No. Commit it then to the flames. For it can contain nothing but sophistry and illusion."

David Hume, *Enquiry Concerning Human Understanding* (1748)

"... philosophy agrees only on its disagreements. In consequence, the history of ... philosophy, unlike the history of other sciences, consists less of a gradual accumulation of knowledge, than of a series of unsuccessful attempts to solve the general riddles of nature and life by 'pure' thought, without the help of ... experience."

"The outcome of philosophy ... was a declaration of its own impotence."

Joseph Dietzgen, *The Nature of Human Brain Work* (1869)

"Philosophical speculations are often nothing but verbal deductions from names and definitions."

Alexander B. Johnson, *A Treatise on Language* (1836)

CHAPTER III. PHILOSOPHY

In this chapter we shall describe and criticize ideas belonging to the second basic class of truth-claims, philosophy. Our main purpose is to distinguish them clearly from religious and scientific ideas or statements.

A. The Origin of Philosophy

Philosophy first appears in each country when a few brilliant pioneers begin to doubt and question traditional religious doctrines. We assume, of course, that these pioneer critics are not converts to a new religion and that they are free to express their new opinions. Western philosophy began in Greece in the fifth century B.C. The first Greek criticism of religion may have been due to the growth of cities, the increase in the number of educated men, contact with the differing religions of other lands, etc., but it could not have been expressed if the Greeks had not been intellectually more free than earlier peoples. Individual sceptics had undoubtedly appeared earlier in other lands, but they were not free to announce their views publicly. Ancient Greece was celebrated and influential because her pioneer sceptics were the first who felt free to state their doubts to their students and because these students and their immediate descendants were wise and tolerant enough to preserve and transmit the writings of these early sceptics. Unfortunately, the more heterodox writings were nearly all lost or destroyed by later and more religious descendants. However, we can find references to them in the works of men like Plato, whose writings were preserved because they were more orthodox and religious.

Early Greek philosophers were relatively free to express themselves chiefly because there was no powerful church and priesthood in ancient Greece. In the Greek city states, public officials officiated as priests as a minor part of their public service. They were therefore less zealous and intolerant than full-time professional priests.

We do not mean to imply that all early philosophers were critical of orthodox religious ideas. In every age, educated men who defend traditional religious beliefs are better paid, more highly honored, and hence more numerous, than those who criticize such beliefs. But men did not need and reward a philosophic defense of conventional religious and social ideas until these ideas had been attacked by the first great critical thinkers. In Europe the first critical thinkers to achieve a place in the history of thought were the pioneer Greek philosophers.

The teaching and development of ancient Greek philosophy continued for a thousand years (600 B.C.-400 A.D.) It is often stated or implied that Plato and Aristotle were the greatest Greek philosophers, but later Greek and Roman thinkers, like the cynics, sceptics, and Epicureans, were much more modern and scientific. Plato and Aristotle have been venerated for 2300 years partly because their writings could be used to defend religion. Greek philosophy was influential for a thousand years because the Greeks and Romans were relatively free intellectually. It was suppressed by the leaders of the new oriental religion, Christianity. They persecuted all pagan philosophers and burned their books. A thousand years of intellectual stagnation followed. Then the men of the renaissance rediscovered the Greek and Roman writings, and began the great intellectual revolution which has produced modern science and positivism.

During the dark ages (400-1200 A.D.), philosophy did not disappear from Europe, but it was studied only by priests who used it to support Christian dogmas. They relied partly upon the more conservative ideas of Plato and Aristotle. Not until the renaissance did secular thinkers become acquainted with the far more advanced ideas of the atomists, cynics, sceptics, and Epicureans, or wih the less orthodox theories of Plato and Aristotle.

In the last 800 years, Western philosophy has passed through three stages of development. It began as a defense of religion, an effort to support revealed truth by appeals to reason. The second stage, the golden age of modern philosophy, was a period in which the leading philosophers believed they used the only sound method of arriving at truth. In this period they increasingly dared to reject revealed truth when considered contrary to reason, though in the beginning they were hesitant about making this clear, and they claimed to have discovered important new truths such as the theory of natural rights and the categorical imperative. This period began with Bruno, burned at the stake in Rome by the Inquisition in 1600, and lasted to about 1850.

The last and shortest stage in the history of philosophy is that in which the leading men called philosophers have devoted themselves chiefly to the study and defense of science. They often call their philosophy the philosophy of science or scientific philosophy. Many of them are more scientists than philosophers. Bertrand Russell and John Dewey are perhaps the leading examples of this third stage of philosophy. They admire and defend science, but retain many philosophic ideas.

One notable difference between religion and philosophy deserves comment. Philosophy appeals chiefly, perhaps exclusively, to educated men. Even in the golden age of Greece, less than 1% of the population used philosophic methods of reasoning. On the other hand, religious ideas and methods of reasoning have been almost universal among common men and predominant among educated men in every age. We are devoting as much space to philosophy as to religion in this book because philosophic reasoning has attracted many of the ablest and most famous thinkers, not because it has ever been dominant among laymen.

B. *Definition of Philosophy*

1. *Previous Usage*

It is typical of modern philosophers that they cannot agree even roughly on the definition of the word *philosophy*. The ancient Greeks seem to have used it as virtually synonymous with abstract non-technological theory. Thus Aristotle distinguished between physics and metaphysics, but included both, and all his writings on individual sciences, under the general term *philosophy*. This broad usage of the term *philosophy* continued until recent times. When the social sciences first began to be created in the 19th Century, they were usually taught by professors of moral philosophy. Some universities still have professors of natural philosophy as well as professors of moral philosophy. We believe that such a broad definition of the term *philosophy* makes it almost useless today, and most philosophers have abandoned this definition.

While the noun, *philosophy*, was long used to cover nearly all general theories, the growth of science since 1500 has taken one group of problems after another away from philosophy. Today, it is difficult for philosophers to find any significant problems which do not belong to some science. Most philosophers still claim metaphysics, which is supposed to deal with the ultimate nature of things, epistemology, which is supposed to tell how we know anything, logic, the theory of what verbal statements are consistent, aesthetics, the theory of what is beautiful, and ethics, the theory of what is morally good. Some philosophers also claim one or more of the following fields:—natural religion, rational psychology, speculative cosmology, rational jurisprudence, the philosophy of the state, the philosophy of history, the general assumptions of science, the synthesis of all scientific conclusions, the philosophy of education, etc. Indeed, the phrase, *the philosophy of*, can be, and has been, set before the name of almost every subject. It frequently means or denotes the basic or general theory of some science.

It is often stated or implied that a person is a philosopher because he is able to take disappointments philosophically, i.e., without the usual complaints and emotional reaction. This idea goes back to ancient times, when some philosophers taught that such conduct is admirable. However, priests and scientists have often recommended the same behavior. It is the reasoning behind such behavior which may be philosophic, and similar reasoning behind the opposite kind of behavior may be equally philosophic. Hence, we should not say that men are philosophers because they "behave philosophically."

Another common error concerning the definition of philosophy is the idea that optimism or pessimism is always a philosophy. Thin people tend to be melancholy and pessimistic, fat people to be cheerful and optimistic, but for physiological rather than rational reasons. Some may try to rationalize their natural feelings by means of philosophy but it is only the rationaliziation, not the personal feeling, which can be philosophic, and it may also be religious, pseudo-scientific, or scientific.

2. *A New Definition*

We shall use the term *philosophy* to denote all conclusions on any subject which have been created and supported by means of philosophic reasoning, plus all philosophic arguments in favor of these and other conclusions. We believe there may be religious, philosophic, and scientific theories on almost any subject. Moreover, theories first supported by religious or scientific reasoning may later be defended with philosophic reasoning and *vice versa.* However, philosophic conclusions and arguments are most common today in publications dealing with the problems still claimed by most philosophers, namely those in metaphysics, epistemology, logic, aesthetics, and ethics.

Philosophic reasoning is deductive, like religious reasoning, but philosophers begin with major premises derived from their own thinking rather than from revelation. In this respect, philosophers and theologians both differ radically from scientists. The latter begin with observation and reject major premises obtained from reason or revelation.

Although philosophers create their own basic premises or truths, they do not believe that these premises are arbitrary or personal. Rather they claim that these truths are disclosed by reason, right reason, the pure light of reason, absolute reason, etc. They treat them as innate or *a priori* ideas which are so common and so obviously true and rational that they must be accepted as the basis of all conclusions. Thus philosophers attribute to reason or rational intuition the kind of axioms and major premises which theologians attribute to revelation.

Most philosophers believe that reason has revealed certain definitions as well as certain major principles or premises to them. Moreover, their conclusions are often implicit in their definitions. That is why they argue so much over definitions. A change in a definition of *god, spirit, matter, existence,* etc., may radically change the conclusions deduced from statements containing it. Arguments over definitions are purely verbal when definitions are recognized as arbitrary, but when definitions are revealed by reason, or are essential to desired factual conclusions, arguments over them become vital and decisive to philosophers. This sharply distinguishes philosophy from science, for scientists know that definitions are arbitrary and cannot support factual conclusions.

In philosophy, *reason*, and *rational* do not mean what they mean in science. The scientist thinks an argument is rational or appeals to reason when it is sound, which means usually that it appeals to relevant facts. The philosopher thinks an argument is reasonable or rational when it ignores relevant facts and appeals to "right reason." Thus Whitehead explains that "it is a great mistake to conceive of this . . . revolt [the rise of science] as an appeal to reason." Rather, it was "an anti-intellectualist movement" because it called for "contemplation of brute fact." When philosophers appeal to reason, they are asking us to ignore the facts and be scientifically unreasonable. Since we have stressed the appeal of philosophers to reason, we shall try to use *reason* and *rational* only as the philosophers use them.

The conflict between science and religion has often been called the conflict between reason and faith. Here *reason* is used in the scientific, not the philosophic sense. Since philosophy relies on pure reason, it is the conflict between anti-religious philosophy and religion, not that between science and religion, which might better be called the conflict between reason and faith.

Most philosophers believe that the conclusions they deduce logically from rational premises are not only formally valid but factually true. If they did not so believe, they would not offer their ethical conclusions as guides to conduct.

Since they believe that every formally valid conclusion from rational premises is true, they must believe that the rational premises obtained by personal intuition or insight are themselves factual truths. However, they are unwilling to submit these premises to verification. They believe that, if a premise is obtained by rational intuition, this alone suffices to prove that the premise is factually true. But modern philosophers try to intuit, or at least use, only unverifiable premises because they fear being ridiculed if their intuitions can be proven to be factually false. Thus most modern philosophic premises are meaningless. But this was not always so. Many earlier philosophers intuited meaningful rational premises and deduced from them philosophic conclusions later proven to be verifiably false.

Philosophers believe not only that deductive reasoning from rational truths can yield factual truths, but also that the first or major premise of a deductive syllogism is the reason why the conclusion is true. If one asks why John is mortal, they reply that he is mortal because all men are mortal. Indeed many adults who are not philosophers, but who have been influenced by them, answer scientific questions thus, especially the questions of children.

Actually, of course, the major premise of deductive syllogism does not explain why the conclusion is true. If true, it is merely a generalization of individual facts, including the conclusion drawn from it. That is why deductive reasoning always begs the apparent factual question. A summary of individual facts requires explanation as much as any fact which it summarizes. Nevertheless, philosophers have been explaining individual facts for 2500 years by restating them in a more general or summary form.

A similar error is to ascribe a "quality" to a class of objects, and then explain that an object in this class has a certain effect *because* it has this quality. The most famous illustration of this typical philosophic practice is the explanation that opium makes one sleepy because it has a dormitive power. Fortunately, the error is more obvious in this form.

G. H. Lewes (1817-78), an early and able positivist, thought that it is possible and useful to create a scientific metaphysics by eliminating unreal or unsolvable questions, those "not amendable to experiment," and by using the scientific method to solve the remaining metaphysical questions. Paradoxically, he also argued that verification is "the grand characteristic distinguishing Science from Philosophy . . ."

If this is true, and we believe it is, problems which suggest verifiable solutions are scientific rather than metaphysical, for metaphysics is traditionally a part of philosophy.

Actually, those philosophers who have claimed that all knowledge is based upon experience, the empirical philosophers, have nearly always arrived at a variety of philosophic conclusions not based upon experience. Indeed that is why they are called philosophers. Had they dealt solely with problems which can be solved by observation and experiment, they would have been called scientists.

If our definition of philosophy is adopted, one should never speak of scientific metaphysics, scientific philosophy, and philosophy of science, or the philosophy of any special science, such as economics or jurisprudence. Philosophy and science are mutually incompatible. No argument can be both philosophic and scientific. The idea of scientific philosophy is as contradictory and meaningless as the idea of a square circle.

Apologists of philosophy and/or religion often claim that everyone has a philosophy and/or religion regardless of whether he knows it. They seek to win an argument by begging the question. In other words, they define philosophy or religion so that it includes all general theories, including those of anti-philosophic and anti-religious scientists, and then claim they have proven that scientists must be philosophic or religious.

The question of whether philosophy includes science is a purely verbal one. The important non-verbal question is whether scientists reason like philosophers. We have argued that philosophers and scientists use different methods of creating truth-claims. To make this point, we have had to define philosophy and science. All definitions are arbitrary and these terms can be redefined so as to make our conclusion false, but this would merely beg the non-verbal question at issue.

3. *The Influence of Mathematics on Philosophy*

We have defined philosophy as alleged factual truth-claims achieved by means of deduction from major premises revealed by pure reason. This method of reasoning may have been first suggested to philosophers by mathematicians, who had found it remarkably productive. Greek geometers, for instance, began their work with definitions and axioms which they thought were revealed to them by reason rather than by observation, and they arrived by deduction at conclusions which they believed to be factual or scientific truths. Most of the early Greek philosophers were trained in geometry and greatly admired it. As a result, they learned to apply the method of geometry to the problems of philosophy. Philosophers were strongly influenced by geometry for 2000 years. When Spinoza wrote his *Ethics,* he stated his axioms and inferences as if he were writing a book on geometry.

We know today that Greek geometers arrived at conclusions which could be used to describe phenomena only because their axioms were based upon observation rather than upon reason. But this vital fact was not stated until the 19th century, when mathematicians finally proved that various systems of non-Euclidian geometry based upon non-Euclidian axioms are possible. Today, geometricians must choose among alternative axioms, and there is no one set of axioms which is more rational than another. One set may be more useful than another, but this can only be determined by experiment, not by reason. Every properly developed system of geometry is self-consistent, but very few are useful in creating verifiable or scientific statements, and whether they are useful can be determined only by observation.

John Stuart Mill, a brilliant pioneer positivist, knew that the great achievements of mathematicians are thought to prove that factual conclusions can be obtained by purely deductive reasoning. He therefore tried to prove that mathematical conclusions are based upon observation rather than rational deduction. Unfortunately, he did not distinguish between verifiable and unverifiable mathematical conclusions. He was unfamiliar with non-Euclidian geometry and did not realize that many valid mathematical conclusions fail to describe what men observe. For this and other less logical reasons, most later thinkers, including some positivists, have rejected Mill's vital conclusion that true mathematical conclusions are based upon observation. However, our analysis of mathematics shows that Mill was largely correct.

4. *Philosophy Does Not Include Logic or Formal Truths*

Logic is one of the last major subjects still claimed by most philosophers. Even logical positivists usually treat logic as part of philosophy. In our opinion, however, this is unwise.

Modern logicians divide logic into two parts, deductive logic and inductive logic, but these differ radically. Deduction proves a conclusion is valid, i.e., implicit in the major premise. Induction proves that a conclusion is true, i.e., verified. Hence, they ought not to be called by the same name, *logic.* What is now called inductive logic is a part of statistics, which in turn is a part of scientific methodology. Many writers on logic have in fact used *scientific method* as a synonym for *inductive logic.* This implies that the theory of scientific method is a part of philosophy and should be taught by men who do not use it and who claim that it should not be used by others to solve the most important problems, those of personal conduct. We can avoid these absurd implications by taking inductive logic out of logic and philosophy and assigning it to science.

Deductive logic, the theory of how to deduce valid conclusions from true, false, or meaningless premises, also belongs to science because its principles are verifiable. It is always possible to prove by observation that a conclusion correctly deduced from true premises is true, and *vice versa.* Hence, the principles of deduction applied in correct deduction must be true.

Correct deductive reasoning may be used to support conclusions which are true, false, or meaningless. Such reasoning proves only that the conclusion is implicit in the premises. But this is not what the conclusion claims. The conclusion states that one symbol is related to another as stated, or that a verbal statement is true. For instance, the syllogism,

'All men are mortal,
John is a man,
John is mortal.'

does not prove that John is mortal. It merely proves that this conclusion is implied by the premises. *But this is not what the conclusion states!* Every deductive conclusion states a claim which has not been proved by stating its premises. This is one reason why men have been so long misled by deductive religious and philosophic reasoning.

Some modern positivists say that there are two kinds of truth, formal and factual. The conclusion of a valid deductive syllogism or mathematical demonstration is called a formal truth because it is the result of formally (logically) correct deductive reasoning. Scientific truths, the conclusions of sound inductive reasoning, are said to be factual truths. On the basis of this distinction, it is asserted or implied that philosophy consists of formal truths, science of factual truths. We disagree.

Every possible declarative statement may be transformed into the conclusion of a valid deductive syllogism. It is only necessary to formulate the missing major and minor premises required to complete the syllogism, and the rules of deductive logic indicate how this may be done in every case. It is not necessary that either of the premises be factually true. The conclusion of any valid deductive syllogism is formally true, according to the theory we are disputing. But if every declarative statement is, or can be made, formally true, the term *formally true* becomes meaningless. There are no formally untrue statements to compare them with.

For these reasons, we believe that the term *formal truth* should be abandoned. It may be meaningful to say that a conclusion is formally consistent with certain premises, but it is misleading to claim that it is therefore formally true. Hence it is unwise to claim that philosophy consists of formal truths.

Our analysis of the term *formal truth* applies also to the term *truth by definition.* The opposite of every truth by definition can be made such a truth by formulating a suitable definition. Since all definitions are arbitrary, all truths by definition are arbitrary. We believe that the term *truth* should be restricted to statements which are not arbitrary, and to statements whose opposites are not equally true. Instead of saying that a conclusion is true by definition, we should say it is consistent with or implicit in a specific definition.

5. *The History and Scientific Criticism of Philosophy are not Philosophy*

Philosophy as we have defined it does not include statements concerning the history of philosophy. The theory that reality is ideal (or material) is meaningless, but the statement that Plato wrote that reality is real is verifiable. All verifiable statements about the history of ideas, including religious and philosophic ideas, belong to science.

Nor does philosophy include scientific criticism of philosophy. Philosophic criticism of philosophic, or any other, theories is a part of philosophy. Scientific criticism of any theory is a part of science. Such criticism includes only meaningful assertions. If a writer who criticizes philosophy is a philosopher for this reason, a man who criticizes astrology is an astrologer.

Moreover, scientific theories as to why most men are religious or philosophic, or both, are a part of science. Like astrology, religion and philosophy have influenced millions of men for thousands of years, and therefore deserve careful scientific study. But the scientific study of philosophy does not produce philosophy. Thus the conclusions stated in this chapter are not philosophic or a part of philosophy. The fact that we deal with religion and philosophy is irrelevant. It is the method of treatment, not the subject matter, which determines whether a theory is a part of religion, philosophy, or science as we define these terms.

6. *Comments on Other Positivistic Definitions of Philosophy*

Having given our own definition of philosophy, we turn now to comment briefly on the definitions of *philosophy* offered by other positivists and philosophers.

Comte called the second of his three stages of intellectual evolution the metphysical rather than the philosophic stage, and he distinguished this stage from the other two by its methods of explaining phenomena, rather than by the methods of creating truth peculiar to it. For him, the metaphysical stage is that in which phenomena are explained as due to abstract forces present in, but independant of, physical objects. In his day, chemists explained the formation of chemical substances as due to inherent predisposing "affinities," and Comte denounced this as pure metaphysics. Our definition of philosophy includes such ideas because of their origin, not their content, but it also covers many other doctrines. In fact it includes most traditional nonreligious ethical, aesthetic, and epistemological doctrines.

Comte used the term *philosophy* to designate any general system of human ideas—religious, metaphysical, or scientific. We use it to denote truth-claims obtained in a certain way, by deduction from rational premises.

Wm. James, who called himself a radical empiricist but failed to be consistently empirical, defined philosophy as "the reflection of man on his relations with the universe." He thought the philosopher could recognize rational philosophic ideas "by certain subjective marks with which it affects him . . . A strong feeling of ease, peace, rest is one of them."

The term, *man's relation to the universe* is certainly *highly* ambiguous and probably meaningless. We cannot find the referent. James himself made no verifiable statement about it. It seems to be a typical philosophic term. Moreover, the test of philosophic truth suggested is useless since an idea which makes one man feel peaceful and rested may cause alarm to other men. For most men, of course, conventional ideas seem peaceful and restful, but what is conventional in one country or social class may not be conventional in others.

For A. J. Ayer, a brilliant contemporary positivist, philosophy is a "department of logic" because it consists of definitions and the formal consequences of definitions. He thinks that philosophers have long dealt largely, if not chiefly, with definitions and their formal implications and that therefore his proposed definition of philosophy is justified by traditional practice as well as by modern theory. We cannot agree. Traditionally, logic is but one of several departments of philosophy. To redefine philosophy as a department of logic would be most confusing.

Regardless of how extensively philosophers have studied definitions and their formal consequences, such analysis has never been their chief or chacteristic activity. Their chief endeavour has always been to create or discover factual truths about man and his world by philosophic reasoning. Such reasoning involves the use of definitions, as do religious and scientific reasoning, but formal logical analysis has never been either the chief basis or the chief intended result of philosophic reasoning. Philosophers claim to begin with innate ideas or "reason" and they arrive at what they believe to be significant factual conclusions. They use formal logical analysis, but so do scientists.

Ayer has also argued that philosophy is a separate study with its own distinctive truths because "the propositions that are expressed in such a [positivist] book as this *[Language, Truth, and Logic]* do fall into a special category." It would be equally reasonable to argue that the arguments in a book against astrology fall into a special category and prove that astrology is a distinct and useful study.

Arthur Pap follows Ayer in rejecting what they both call "speculative philosophy" and we call philosophy, but he thinks that philosophers can still function usefully by analyzing logically the concepts, methods, and pre-suppositions of science. Like Ayer, he believes that philosophers have often practiced such analysis. He includes in philosophy that part of logic, ethics, aesthetics, mathematics, and science which deals with the analysis of concepts. Thus for him philosophy is not merely a division of logic, as Ayer teaches.

We can see no reason why scientists need call upon outsiders, the philosophers, to supply them with definitions, methods, or presuppositions. Rather we are convinced that scientists are better qualified to define their terms, select and improve their methods, and state their assumptions than any outsiders. To be meaningful and useful, a scientific hypothesis must be verifiable. To create such hypotheses, the scientist must use terms which denote observable things. The selection of such terms and the formulation of such hypotheses is a vital part of the scientist's work. None of it should be delegated to outsiders.

The efforts of able positivists like Ayer and Pap to give a new definition to the ancient term *philosophy* seem to be due to personal psychological and economic motives rather than to pure logical analysis. They have been trained in departments of philosophy on books written by men called philosophers. This has made the term *philosophy* emotionally pleasant. Moreover, they must earn a living by teaching in departments of philosophy, and, to apply for these positions, they must call themselves philosophers.

In 1924 E. A. Burtt published an influential book, *The Metaphysical Foundations of Modern Science,* in which he argued that science requires metaphysical assumptions. He devoted most of this book to a revealing discussion of the metaphysical theories of the great pioneer scientists, from Copernicus to Newton, and then concluded illogically that, since these men accepted some metaphysical ideas, science requires metaphysical assumptions. It would be equally logical to argue that since all of these men were superstitious, in some cases extremely so, modern science must be based upon superstition. It is obviously impossible to prove that a metaphysical theory is a necessary presupposition of science since all such theories are meaningless.

In his book, *In Defense of Philosophy* (1950), M. C. Cornforth, a Marxist, declares that "Everybody has some kind of philosophy. . . . For philosophy is nothing but our most general account of the nature of the world and of our place in it—our world outlook" (p. ix). We have criticized this argument once (p. 116), but it deserves further comment.

If such a general account is meaningful, it is a part of science. Moreover, it will be so clear and prosaic that few people would call it philosophy. For instance, astronomers can briefly describe how men are placed among the stars and planets, and geographers can describe where men are located on the earth, but few philosophers would call this metaphysics. It is too demonstrable and unpoetic. Moreover, chemists and physicists can give us a general account of the basic elements or constituents of the world, but what they say is likewise too sensible and prosaic to be philosophy.

Everyone may have meaningful theories about "the world and our [geographical] place in it," but this is not philosophy. Philosophy consists largely of meaningless, but often poetic, statements about the metaphysical nature of the world and our spiritual place in it. It differs from religion in the methods of demonstration used. Most people have religious rather than philosophic ideas, and some who are not religious are scientific rather than philosophic. Hence, it is very misleading to say that "everyone has some kind of philosophy."

C. A Criticism of Philosophy

Philosophic doctrines, like religious doctrines, can be divided into two classes, verifiable in theory and all others. The former are false if they contradict scientific truths and superfluous if they duplicate them. The latter are meaningless.

1. *Verifiable Philosophic Doctrines are False or Superfluous.*

Scientists have again and again proven that certain verifiable philosophic conclusions are false. The conflict between scientists and philosophers has been almost as bitter and important as the conflict between scientists and priests. The prerenaissance students of natural philosophy treated the works of Aristotle as their bible, and the subsequent early progress of science consisted very largely in proving that the verifiable doctrines of Aristotle and other philosophers were false. But this did not discourage philosophers until very recently. Hegel elaborated in great detail the application of philosophy to scientific problems, even though this exposed him to almost immediate refutation at the hands of 19th century scientists. His *Philosophy of Nature* is full of demonstrable errors.

While philosophers have increasingly restricted themselves to unverifiable conclusions, modern philosophers often state verifiable conclusions, usually in some field, such as psychology, where scientific research is new and difficult. For instance, in *Philosophy in a New Key* (1942), Susanne K. Langer concludes that "man is more cruel than any beast" because "animals react only to the deed . . . whereas we . . . employ sanctions, threaten vague penalties and try to forestall offenses by merely exhibiting the symbols of their consequences" (Mentor ed., p. 233). While the conclusion that "man is more cruel than any beast" may be a truth by definition, it looks like a verifiable scentific statement, one which no scientist would make without detailed observation of human and animal behavior, partly under controlled experimental conditions. In fact, if Mrs. Langer's conclusion had been verified before she made it, it would probably be a significant contribution to science. As far as we are aware, it it not now found in textbooks on either psychology or zoology. Moreover, in her book and in the works of other modern philosophers, there are numerous other apparently verifiable scientific claims which, if actually verified, would be notable contributions to science. Indeed, one of the chief attractions of some modern books on philosophy is that they state and support meaningful theories which are as new and/or striking as they are unverified.

2. *Unverifiable Philosophic Doctrines are Meaningless*

As we have explained, all philosophic doctrines are either verifiable or unverifiable in theory. The former can often be proven false, and scientists are learning to refute more and more of them. Hence, philosophers are becoming reluctant to use philosophic reasoning to create verifiable theories. On the other hand, conclusions for which no method of verification can be conceived are meaningless. It does not matter practically whether they are considered true or false. We shall now illustrate this reasoning by applying it individually to some of the most important traditional problems and principles of philosophy. We begin with those of metaphysics.

a. Metaphysics

(1) *Are there Noumena Behind Phenomena?*

Perhaps the most basic of all modern questions is that as to whether sensations (phenomena) are caused by independent objects or events, or whether they are created by the individual person. Most philosophers have assumed or argued that phenomena have independant unobservable causes, which they call *noumena* or *ultimate reality*. Since scientists cannot observe noumena, philosophers have discussed them repeatedly and extensively. They have in fact created numerous and astonishingly diverse theories about noumena.

The question of whether phenomena are caused by noumena is distinct from and prior to the question of how noumena should be described. If there are noumena, one may ask many questions about them, but the first thing to decide is whether the term *noumena* has any referents, i.e., whether it is meaningful.

All referents of meaningful nouns are by definition observable. Since noumena are by definition unobservable, the noun *noumena* cannot have any referents and is therefore meaningless.

For this reason some positivists have called themselves phenomenalists, or have been so described by their critics. However, *phenomenalism* is an ambiguous term. If it means only the theory that *noumena* is a meaningless word, all positivists are phenomenalists. If, however, it includes also the theory that phenomena are subjective and have no independent causes, positivists are not phenomenalists. Since different men observe the same objects and events, their sensations must have independent, non-subjective causes. But this does not prove that phenomena are caused by noumena. It is senseless to speak of unobservable causes. To be meaningful, we must conclude that phenomena are due to observable causes. *Observable* should be defined to mean "capable of causing a sensation." Then the things and events which men sense are observable (sensible) and are also independent of the observor.

Although philosophers have defined *phenomenon* as the effect produced upon the senses by a *noumenon*, they often speak of observing or sensing phenomena. This practice is so common that it sounds extremely awkward to speak of "having a phenomenon" instead of "observing a phenomena." Yet the latter phrase clearly implies that phenomena are the causes of sensations, not the results of observing noumena. One senses the cause of sensation, not the sensation itself. For this reason, and the others previously noted, it would probably be well to abandon the terms *phenomena* and *noumena.*

The philosopher Berkeley assumed that qualities are separate from things and argued that men perceive only qualities. This resembles the theory that men observe phenomena, not things. Berkeley's argument is senseless because nouns like *quality, color, sound,* and *substance* (unqualified substance) have no referents. We perceive qualified objects and events, not qualities or unqualified substances.

(2) *How should Noumena be Described*

If one believes that phenomena are caused by noumena, a host of typically philosophic questions may be asked. Are noumena real or unreal; changing or unchanging; uniform, dualistic, or pluralistic; ideal or material; and so forth? All such questions are meaningless. Since noumena are unobservable, it is impossible to conceive of any method of verifying answers to problems about them. Whether any answer is true or false does not matter; i.e., it does not state or imply what we can or will observe or experience. The same analysis applies of course to all questions about reality, ultimate reality, or any other unobservable metaphysical entities.

Many philosophers not only claim that unobservable noumena are real but that observable things are unreal. This theory is implicit in the common philosophic distinction between appearances and reality.

Real and *unreal* are ambiguous. *Real* may be defined as metaphysically real (self-existent, unchanging, permanent, etc.) or as non-imaginary. The former definition is senseless; the latter sensible. Thus the question of whether noumena are real may seem to be meaningful because the adjective *real* may be interpreted to signify non-imaginary. However, this is not the way philosophers use *real.* If *real* is a synonym for non-imaginary, appearances are obviously much more real than any unobservable reality, for one can prove by observation that most appearances are not imaginary.

It should be especially noted that we have *not* said that the problem of whether there is a separate reality behind appearance is insoluble. A meaningless problem can be neither soluble nor insoluble. In the past, advanced thinkers often called philosophic problems insoluble. Logical positivists emphasize the fact that they are senseless and absurd rather than insoluble.

The problem of whether there is an unobservable reality behind appearance may seem sensible to some because it resembles or suggests the meaningful question as to whether conclusions based on first appearances, or on incomplete data, are as reliable as those based on all appearances.

Scientists are well aware that new data, new appearances, may require a revision of previous conclusions. But this is entirely different from the meaningless philosophic theory that there is a reality behind all appearances not revealed by these appearances. Unfortunatley, philosophic theories often seem meaningful because they resemble or suggest meaningful ideas.

Christian philosophers have long taught that reality is dualistic, consisting of both matter and spirit. In reaction against this orthodox dogma, many thinkers have asserted that reality is monistic, consisting only of a single substance. However, they erred in taking the problem seriously. Since it is quite senseless, all answers to it are meaningless. Hence, logical positivists are not monists.

Pluralism sounds more scientific than monism or dualism because the world is obviously full of an infinite variety of things. Some modern positivistic thinkers, like John Dewey, have therefore called themselves pluralists. This is a mistake because pluralism is a theory about reality, not about appearances, and all theories about unobservables are meaningless. Moreover, it is so obvious that appearances are plural that it is pointless to say so.

If one assumes a monistic reality behind appearances, the next metaphysical question is whether this reality is material or ideal. This problem is non-sensical and nonsignificant not only because it uses *reality*, a senseless term, but because the adjectives *material* and *ideal* are also meaningless.

When we say that olive trees have green leaves, the hearer can verify our statement because he understands it. But when we say olive trees are ideal or material, he can not verify the statement because he does not know what we mean.

To explain what a word means, one must point to a thing or event it denotes or describes, or define it in terms which can be so explained. The adjective *green* is meaningful because one can point to green things, but *ideal* and *material* are meaningless because we cannot point to ideal or material things.

Moreover, it is pointless to say that everything is ideal or material. Adjectives are meaningful and useful only when they enable us to distinguish between one thing and another. If everything were colored the same shade of green, no one would know what *colored* or *green* meant.

The metaphysical doctrine that ultimate reality is material is called materialism. It is entirely different from the theory that chemical elements consist of matter, defined scientifically, because it is possible to observe these elements and determine what they consist of. Unfortunately, the term *materialism* has been used to name both theories, and philosophers have been so confused thereby that they have often argued that scientific research in nuclear physics has disproven the philosophic theory of materialism. Actually, scientific research cannot prove or refute any philosophic theory. The correct argument against philosophic materialism is that it is senseless because it is a philosophic theory.

One of the reasons why the philosophic issue of idealism versus materialism has seemed meaningful is that it has been confused with the issue of whether certain scientific theories of materialism are true. Another reason is that the term *ideal* has been confused with the term *mental*. In other words, some philosophers have assumed that the statement that phenomena are mental means that they are ideal. This is an error because metaphysics claims to deal with the unobservable noumena behind phenomena, and the metaphysical term *ideal* can be applied only to these noumena and not to phenomena or appearances. Thus the fact that phenomena are mental does not mean or imply that metaphysical noumena or ultimate realities are ideal.

(3) *Does the Universe or Life Have a Purpose?*

One of the most debated problems of philosophy is whether the universe has a purpose. This question is senseless because the noun *universe* is referentless and imageless and therefore cannot be used in answers for which a method of verification can be conceived.

This noun may be verbally defined in many ways. Let us consider two verbal definitions: (1) the sum of all existing things, (2) the sum of all observable things. The former definition cannot be illustrated by pointing because it presumably includes some unobservable things. The latter can be illustrated by pointing at everything but this makes it meaningless. A noun is useful only when it distinguishes one or more things from other things. All meaningful statements are true of some things but not of everything. No statement about everything can be verified by observation.

The noun *purpose* is questionable, but this is a minor point since the question can easily be restated as, "Is the universe purposive?" Much more serious is the fact that both versions of the question suggest that inanimate things can be purposive. Since this adjective has been defined by pointing to animal behavior, it should not be applied to non-animal behavior. To ask whether the stars are purposive is as inappropriate as to ask whether a stone is loving. Of course one can claim that the universe is an animal, but this is either false or senseless.

The metaphysician may reply that although he asks literally whether the universe has a purpose he is really talking about the ultimate reality behind appearances, not the visible universe. However, we have already explained that the term *ultimate reality* is meaningless. Hence, all questions about it are senseless.

Another variation of our question asks whether life has a purpose. It is meaningless because the noun *life* is meaningless, i.e., it cannot be defined directly or indirectly by pointing. Moreover, only individual animals can be purposeful and life is certainly not an individual animal.

There are other variants of these questions. Thus philosophers have asked whether life or the universe has a reason or end or excuse, etc. All such questions can easily be shown to be absurd by the same kind of analysis.

It is sometimes asserted that life or the universe must have a purpose because everything has a reason. This argument is plausible because the term *reason* is ambiguous. Among other things, it may be a synonym for *cause,* and scientists believe that everything has a cause. However, philosophers want to believe that life has a reason in the sense of purpose, not a reason in the sense of cause.

Another similar philosophic argument is that life must have a purpose because we could not go on living if life were purposeless. This argument is plausible because the term *life* does not mean the same thing in its two uses here. In its first use, *life* is a synonym for *life in general,* a meaningless concept. In its second, it refers to the life of a given person or persons. Individual persons may want to live longer only when they purpose to do something. But the latter statement, even if true, does not prove that some obscure abstraction called *life* has a purpose.

When a philosopher is told that men can purpose, but life or the universe cannot, he is likely to reply that he is well aware of this obvious truism and is speaking symbolically. Philosophers often treat plain prosaic common sense as inferior to profound symbolic truths. However, the only way to make any figurative statement meaningful is to translate it into a clear and literal statement. We know of no such meaningful translations of the above questions.

(4) *Is the Universe Finite or Infinite*

Scientists as well as philosophers have discussed this

question. It is senseless for two reasons. The noun *universe* is all-inclusive and therefore useless, as explained above. The adjectives *finite* and *infinite* are also meaningless, because the former is all-inclusive and the latter is non-inclusive. *Finite* may be defined by pointing to everything, which makes it all-inclusive, but *infinite* cannot be defined by pointing to anything.

Some modern physicists seem to imply that pure mathematical reasoning can solve the problem of whether the universe is spatially finite or infinite. This is a gross error. All purely mathematical reasoning begs the question at issue by using arbitrary axioms and definitions which make the conclusion inevitable. Moreover, such reasoning cannot yield factual conclusions. The fact that the terms *finite* and *infinite* have been given useful formal definitions by mathematicians does not make them factually meaningful.

The question of whether the universe is infinite includes the much discussed question of whether it is temporally infinite, i.e., whether it has a first cause and/or a definite beginning. But the phrase *temporally infinite* is senseless. No one has ever observed a first cause of anything, and it is impossible to conceive of any observation or experiment which would prove that any object had a first cause.

All scientific observation of causes supports the conclusion that every cause has one or more causes. Failure to find a cause can never prove that no cause can be found; it can at most prove that no cause has yet been found.

On the other hand, the scientific principle that every cause has a cause does not prove that the universe has a cause. This principle applies only to individual causes or events, not to any collection of events or objects like the history of man or the universe. It implies that a collection of numerous events and objects has numerous causes, not that it has a single cause, and a first cause is a single cause.

Some modern astronomers seem to think that they can determine by scientific observation whether what they call the universe (a group of observed galaxies) began or came into being suddenly out of nothing at a certain date or whether it has always existed (been observable). Thus certain of them have argued that the universe must have begun at an estimated date because it has been expanding at a known rate and this expansion must have begun at a definite time. However, the fact that observed galaxies may have been moving away from each other does not prove that myriads of unobserved galaxies have been doing the same, nor that if they have there must have been a time when they and their movement arose out of nothing. The idea of creation out of nothing is a senseless philosophic idea, and scientists cannot verify such theories. They may not know why or when galaxies began to move apart, but the fact that they do not know this does not support a meaningless philosophic explanation.

(5) *Do Men Exist?*

René Descartes (1596-1650), one of the founders of modern Western philosophy, explicitly rejected all prior religion and philosophy and tried to build up a new philosophy by pure rational or philosophic reasoning. He began by asserting that, in order to doubt previous doctrines, one must think. He then asserted that from the promise 'I think' one can conclude that 'I am.' Thus he claimed to prove that men exist. His brief argument 'I think, therefore I am' is one of the most celebrated in the entire history of philosophy. It is therefore worth noting that it is quite illogical and invalid, even as pure deductive logic, because he has stated only a minor premise and a conclusion. To complete the deductive syllogism and validate his conclusion, one must add the appropriate major premise. 'Men who think are men who are.' To make his conclusion philosophically true as well as logically valid, one must go on and assert that this major premise is a result of logical intuition, i.e., is revealed by the clear light of reason. Descartes neither stated nor validated this necessary major premise. Hence his conclusion was not the result of valid philosophic reasoning.

But the chief criticism om Descartes' conclusion, on which he based his whole philosophy, is not that it is philosophically invalid but that both it and the missing major premise are literally senseless. What does it mean to say that men are or exist? Descartes did not explain what he meant, but we may be sure that, as a philosopher, he was trying to prove that he existed metaphysically, not physically. This is unverifiable and meaningless. One can arbitrarily define *physically existing* to mean *observable* and then prove that a thing is observable, but no metaphysical thing or event can be observable.

We have noted that the missing major premise in Descartes' basic syllogism is 'men who think are men who exist.' This is a typical meaningless identity statement. The literature of philosophy contains many others—knowledge is virtue, truth is beauty, virtue is beauty, the world is will, nature is God, death is life, etc. Such statements are usually inconsistent with accepted definitions of the terms used. They can be made formally valid by agreeing on new definitions, and the philosophers who support them often argue for such new definitions, but whether they are formally valid is irrelevant. If no method of verifying them can be conceived, and none have been, they are senseless. Yet such statements are often considered profound and important.

(6) *Does a God Exist?*

For reasons already noted, the vast majority of philosophers have been religious and have tried to use philosophic reasoning to support religious dogmas. We call these arguments philosophic rather than religious because we are more interested in the method of reasoning than in the subject matter. We cannot spare the space required to review all the philosophic arguments for all religious dogmas, but we can criticize some of those alleged to prove that a supreme being or god exists.

The ontological proof claims that men have the idea of a perfect being, that existence is one of the qualities of a perfect being and that therefore such a person must exist. It is unsound because, (1) it uses several meaningless words—*perfect, existence qualities, exist* and (2) it assumes that definitions or ideas determine what is factually true. It would be equally logical to argue that men have the idea of a perfect society or utopia, that existence is one of the qualities of a utopia, and that therefore utopia exists.

The first-cause proof asserts that every finite thing has a cause, that the universe is finite, and that therefore it must have a cause. Moreover, it must have a first cause since infinite regress is impossible. This proof is unsound because it uses senseless terms—*universe, infinite* and *finite;* because it asserts the universe has a single cause; and because it denies infinite regress without evidence. We discussed these points a few pages back, and need not repeat this discussion here.

The natural-law argument claims that natural laws imply a supreme lawgiver. It is based upon a false analogy between human and natural laws. Human laws are established and enforced by men, but natural laws are mere descriptions of what has been observed. When men disobey a human law, the police try to catch and punish them, but when they "disobey a natural law" the law is revised to fit the new observations.

The order-in-the universe proof, closely related to the previous proof, asserts that the universe is orderly, rational, harmonious, etc., and that hence there must be a supreme person who has created this order. However, if everything is orderly, the word *orderly* is senseless, and if some parts of the universe are disorderly, the argument is unsound.

Moreover, if the universe is so rational that it must have had a creator, why cannot we argue with equal logic that this creator must be even more rational and therefore must have an even greater creator? To assume that the universe has a cause, and its creator none, is illogical and question-begging.

The similar argument-from-design asserts that the world was designed to suit men and that, consequently, there must be a supreme designer. It has been refuted by the theory of evolution, which makes clear that natural selection has produced men fitted to live in a previously existing world. Moreover, men are often injured by natural events. Evolution has not yet created any people perfectly fitted to their environment.

Another version of the argument-from-design asserts that, just as the existence of a watch implies the existence of a watchmaker, so the existence of man implies a divine mechanic. This argument depends entirely upon the comparison of men with watches, i.e., upon the assumption that men are mechanisms. To refute this argument, we need only point out that men are organisms, not mechanisms, and hence they do not imply a divine mechanic.

If an organism implied a maker, it would be unnecessary to compare man to a mechanism. This comparison implies that the one who makes it recognizes that an organism does not suggest a divine maker. The conclusion that man has a maker, therefore, is here entirely dependent upon the claim that man is a mechanism. Yet the men who make this claim often criticize scientists for their "mechanical" theories about men.

The idealist proof of the existence of a god asserts that things exist only when they are being observed. Since human observation is intermittent, the idealist argues that there must be an eternal observor, a god, who perceives things steadily and thus enables them to exist steadily.

This is a proof by definition. The idealist first defines

to exist as *to be observed,* and then concludes that things must be observed constantly in order to exist constantly. Such verbal proofs or tautologies are common in the writings of philosophers.

Moreover, if this proof were sound, it would prove that a lone god cannot exist, for there would be no-one to observe him.

The moral proof claims that there would be no such thing as right and wrong if no deity existed. It is unsound because the terms *right* and *wrong* are meaningless when used as moral terms. We shall elaborate this point later (see pp. 187-90).

Some philosophers have sought to avoid all arguments concerning the existence of a god by defining *god* so that there will be no doubt that this term has a referent. Thus Spinoza defined *god* as that eternal order which underlies all things. Apparently he thought that few men would ever fail to perceive such an order. A modern writer, H. N. Wieman, proclaims explicity that he wants "to prove the existence of God by definition." However, a verbal definition cannot prove anything. Verifiable knowledge comes from observation, not from purely verbal arguments or assertions. Conclusions based upon definitions are not factual truths but mere tautologies.

Definitions which apply the term *god* to something which all can observe inevitably create serious confusion. Whenever an old word is defined in a new way, many people are misled. Moreover, if *god* is redefined to designate something observable by all, it becomes obvious that *god* is not personal, rational, benevolent, wise, etc., for there is no such person or thing which all men can observe.

We have explained the chief objections to the oldest and best-known philosophic arguments used to prove that a supreme being exists. The most important objection to these arguments is that they are unverifiable in theory as well as practice, and therefore literally meaningless, because they use senseless terms like *finite, orderly, rational, existence, first cause,* etc. The logical positivists were the first to state and publicize this criticism.

b. Epistemology

We turn now from problems of metaphysics to those of epistemology, another traditional division of philosophy. The general problem of epistemology is how men can learn anything about the unobservable noumena behind phenomena. All problems as to how men know observable things belong to the scientists. Thus the chief problem of epistemology is artificial and senseless. It is created by the meaningless assumption that sensations have unobservable causes.

There is a school of philosophers who call themselves realists because they believe that appearance and reality are the same, or that appearances reveal reality. This suggests the common sense theory that sensations are caused by observable things. However, it is a philosophic theory because it uses the term *real* philosophicly and therefore states a meaningless proposition. There is no conceivable way of verifying the doctrine that appearance is, or reveals, ultimate reality.

Other philosophers have claimed to solve the epistemological problem by asserting that men are born with true innate or inherited ideas about ultimate reality. Unfortunately, these philosophers cannot agree among themselves as to what these innate ideas are, and they cannot persuade other philosophers that men have innate ideas. Here, as elsewhere, rational intuition and deductive reasoning from intuited ideas results in a multitude of inconsistent conclusions. Apparently those who believe in innate ideas merely use this term to dignify their personal prejudices. Moreover, these prejudices are meaningless if they include senseless terms like *real, ideal, material,* etc.

A third solution of the epistemological problem is the

doctrine that some supernatural power puts true ideas about metaphysical reality in human minds. However, this is merely an evasion of the problem. It is always possible to solve any problem as to how things happen by saying that some spirit makes them happen, but this solution is senseless and often prevents continued search for a useful solution. The assertion that a spirit does anything is senseless because it could not be verified by any conceivable sense data.

There is one problem of knowledge often discussed by epistemologists, the so-called problem of induction, which apparently does not deal with how men know ultimate reality. All induction is based upon observation of appearances, yet philosophers have claimed that there is an epistemological problem in induction because it yields a *universal* conclusion based on a limited number of cases. However, this problem can easily be avoided by qualifying inductive conclusions so that they are not absolute and universal. Most scientists do this, implicitly if not explicitly. Even when they state their theories in universal terms they admit that these theories are only probable truths which will be revised whenever new observations require this. But if an inductive conclusion is only a probable truth, there is no problem of how induction can yield universal truths.

Some philosophers have gone on to claim that induction cannot even yield probable truth. They assert there is no reason to believe the future will be like the past. They mean, of course, that rational intuition does not disclose such a reason. But this is irrelevant to the scientist. He is interested only in whether experience shows that it is wise to assume that the future will be like the past. Fortunately, experience has demonstrated repeatedly that this assumption, on which all applied science rests, is entirely sound. Hence, the assumption has become a truth verified by observation.

It has been claimed by some philosophers that induction cannot be justified by induction because this involves reasoning in a circle. But this is a nihilistic argument which applies equally against all methods of demonstration. No such purely verbal reasoning can offset the fact that induction works in practice. If the inductive argument for induction is circular, a circular argument may be valid. The final justification of every theory, including the theory of induction, is that it can be verified by induction.

In *Science and the Modern World* (1925), A. N. Whitehead asserts that, "Induction presupposes metaphysics," because "you cannot have a rational justification for your appeal to history till your metaphysics has assured you that there *is* a history to appeal to; . . ." (Mentor ed., p. 45). This is a perfect illustration of how nonsensical epistemology is. What docs it matter whether there really, i.e., metaphysically, is a history to appeal to? Would any man be affected in any way if philosophers suddenly discovered that there really is or is not a history, which scientists can study? Does it mean anything to say that "there *is* a history to appeal to" after scientists have already appealed to it with brilliant success?

It is of course possible to state meaningful problems of how men know, but these problems belong to science rather than epistemology. For instance, we may ask which method of statistical analysis is best suited to given scientific data. This is a problem of applied statistics, not an epistemological problem.

Our whole book deals with the most basic problem of how men know, the problem of whether religious philosophic, or scientific reasoning is best. But this is not a problem of epistemology because we are not trying to explain how men know metaphysical reality.

c. *Ethics and Aesthetics*

Philosophy includes two normative studies, ethics and aesthetics. They are called normative because they prescribe norms, rules of conduct. Ethics prescribes what men should do and applaud because it is morally good in itself. Aesthetics prescribes what men should do and appreciate because it is beautiful. These studies are sometimes called normative *sciences,* but this is highly misleading because the problems, principles, and reasoning are philosophic and therefore completely unscientific.

We shall discuss ethics in detail in Chapter V and therefore need say nothing about it here except that all ethical theories are meaningless for much the same reasons that other philosophic theories are meaningless.

While aesthetics is less important practically than ethics, it is a study which has been more completely dominated by philosophers. For thousands of years, ethics has been dominated by religious teachers, but they have written little about aesthetics. Moreover, scientists have as yet worked very little on the problem of why men call some things beautiful. As a result, the writings of art critics, music critics, literary critics and dramatic critics contain an extraordinary amount of philosophic nonsense.

For the philosopher, the basic problem of aesthetics is the problem of what is beautiful, not the problem of why men call some things beautiful. The latter belongs to science, for we can conceive of verifiable answers to it.

Aesthetics is called normative since it sets norms. It tells us what we ought to call beautiful and what we ought to enjoy aesthetically because it is beautiful. It is based logically on the intuited and undebatable axiom that men ought to appreciate absolute beauty just as ethics is based upon the axiom that men ought to act ethicly. Both of these axioms can be explained as analytical conclusions, i.e., as so-called truths by definition, but they are more than this to the philosopher. He regards them as factual truths revealed by reason, as basic statements of what men should do.

We turn now to a few samples of aesthetic theory. The Geman philosopher Schelling, who developed a comprehensive philosophy of art, taught that artistic perception reveals the identity of subject and object. It is the perfect perception by intelligence of its real self in a work of art.

Hegel defined the beautiful as the ideal showing itself to sense or through a sensuous medium. It lives in appearance and takes the form of unity of the manifold.

Charles Léveque thought that beauty is spiritual in nature but takes the form of unity and variety of parts, intensity of color, grace, etc. In living beings, these qualities are perceived by reason to be the manifestations of an invisible vital force. In inorganic nature, these qualities are produced by an immaterial physical force.

We could offer many other samples of philosophic reasoning about the ultimate nature of beauty-in-itself, but these should suffice to suggest how senseless such thinking is. Here, as elsewhere, the conclusions of philosophers are entirely meaningless because no method of verifying them can be conceived. Philosophic terms like *absolute beauty, the beautiful, art, the ideal, spiritual,* etc., do not denote or describe any observable thing. Hence, no-one can understand and test the statements containing them. Whether these statements are true or false does not matter because things remain the same whether they are true or false.

The chief practical result of the fact that aesthetic theory is generally accepted is that students are taught in school that they ought to like certain books, pictures, plays, statues and other artistic works because these things are beautiful. Consequently, obedient students often spend many dull hours trying to enjoy what they do not or cannot enjoy, and some of them entirely give up reading or listening to music because it has not been pleasant.

Since all aesthetic theory is senseless, it cannot help teachers to determine what is beautiful in the sense of agreeable. They accept the dogmas of art critics and these dogmas are either traditional or personal. Even when they are personal and sensible, i.e., based upon agreeable personal sensations, these judgments mislead most students, for what pleases an art critic rarely pleases most students.

The scientific approach to art is entirely different from that of the philosopher. The scientist begins by observing what artists do and how people react to their performances and products. He also observes how people use words like *art* and *beautiful*. On the basis of such observation, he may conclude that every society has different arts and that some individuals like certain art products while other individuals prefer different ones. He does not try to tell people what they ought to like nor does he affirm that the plays of Shakespeare are more beautiful than soap operas. He may discover that people with high I.Q.'s like Shakespeare's plays better than soap opera, or that they merely claim to do so because they have been taught in school that his plays are superior, or that most men call something beautiful when they like it, and ugly when they dislike it. Herbert Spencer suggested that, as a result of evolution, men consider women beautiful when they look as if they would bear and rear strong and intelligent children. These are but a few samples of the kind of conclusions which might result from scientific study of art and of the use of the word *beautiful*. In sharp contrast to the philosophic theories of aesthetics stated previously, they are all verifiable by observation and are therefore meaningful.

D. Why Men Philosophize

We have explained why all philosophic statements are false, superfluous, or meaningless. Nevertheless, many able thinkers have failed to recognize this, have reasoned philosophically, and have believed that the resulting conclusions are true and useful. Why is this so? Why do men still philosophize?

The chief reason is that philosophic reasoning can be

used to support many conclusions that men want to believe. It is possible to support any desired conclusion by philosophizing. All that is necessary is to determine the major premises necessary to validate a desired conclusion, assert that this is an innate idea or an obvious truth of reason, and then deduce the desired conclusion. Since philosophers have no method of agreeing on major premises, one is as philosophically valid as another. Thus philosophic reasoning can support any conclusion that one wishes to believe. Moreover, since any conclusion can be thus validated, the reason why some conclusions are selected and supported rather than others must usually be that men wish to believe these conclusions.

Of course, philosophers usually do not deliberately choose among alternative premises or axioms those which will validate desired conclusions. When they perceive that certain premises will support desired conclusions, they may stop thinking before they have thought of other alternative premises, and, if they should think or read of alternative premises, they will find it easy to forget them because they do not lead to pleasant conclusions. Moreover, a premise which supports such a conclusion seems inherently plausible or logical, and the man who chooses it usually thinks he is choosing it because it is rational, not because it leads to a desired conclusion. However, some philosophers do assert that a premise which leads to a desired conclusion is preferable for that reason alone. They claim that it has spiritual or emotional value, and they assert that it is more important to satisfy men emotionally or spiritually than to be logical or scientific. In other words, they use favorably loaded or meliorative terms to denote wishful thinking and then endorse it.

To illustrate wishful thinking in philosophy, we shall note a few conclusions which philosophers have been most eager to support.

The chief conclusion that men have wanted to support

by philosophizing is the conclusion that some or all of the religious doctrines taught them as children are true. While philosophy began in ancient Greece as a criticism of, or substitute for, religion and while some philosophers in every age have criticized or rejected religion, the great majority have always been eager to support some traditional religious dogmas. This majority includes not only paid religious apologists, like Thomas Acquinas, but men as diverse as Plato and Whitehead, Socrates and Bergson, Leibnitz and Wm. James. Moreover, these men have been much more highly praised by historians and teachers of philosophy than the few who used philosophic reasoning to attack the basic dogmas of religion. Until recently, university faculties of philosophy, especially in America, consisted almost entirely of clergymen or deeply religious laymen. As late at 1860 all fellows at Oxford and Cambridge were ordained Church of England priests, and they selected their successors.

We have already explained why most men want to create and accept religious ideas, and need not repeat them here. But we do wish to note that this explanation also explains in large part why men develop philosophic arguments with which to support and defend religious dogmas.

In the second place, many men want to believe that certain political theories are true. Plato in his *Republic* and Sir Thomas More in his *Utopia* used philosophic reasoning to support many suggested social reforms. It is surprisingly easy to devise a philosophic defense of a reform which one desires for other reasons. Like religion, philosophy can be used both for and against any reform. Thus the philosophic theory of the divine right of kings was used to defend monarchy while the equally meaningless philosophic theory of natural rights was used to attack it. The natural-rights theory has also been used to attack the slave trade, secure votes for women, repeal censorship, laws, etc. It is still an influential argument for and against many proposed reforms. It is a remarkable fact that men who reject sound scientific arguments for needed reforms will often be favorably influenced by the senseless claim that men have a natural right to be free, to vote, to speak, to strike, etc.

While the chief reason men philosophize is that they wish to support their previous prejudices, men have unquestionably tried to create or discover new truths by means of philosophic reasoning. Men have always been curious and have always sought new truths. Until the modern creation and successful demonstration of systematic scientific research, men had no well developed alternative to religious reasoning except philosophic reasoning. It was natural therefore that those who became sceptical of religious revelation should have tried philosophic reasoning. We have already noted how the brilliant achievements of Greek mathematicians made men hopeful of achieving equal successes by philosophic reasoning.

Philosophic reasoning is still attractive to many men because it seems much easier and more pleasant than laborious and often costly scientific research. A philosopher needs only an armchair, a desk, and a convenient public library. A sudden inspiration may seem to enable him to solve a problem which has baffled men for a thousand years. Such solutions have actually made some philosophers very famous.

To develop a sound scientific argument against human slavery, would be a difficult and expensive task. It might require very costly social experiments. How much easier it is to discover that pure reason dictates that all men should be free, that negros are men, and that therefore negros should be free. This is, of course, only one of many possible philosophic arguments against slavery, but all of them are easier to state and prove than the scientific case against slavery.

This explanation of philosophic thinking applies also to religious thinking. In the beginning, religious ideas were created because no one knew how to perform the laborious task of creating scientific ideas, and men desired answers to their questions, but today, when laborious scientific research is widely practised, religious thinking is often evidence that men are intellectually lazy.

Another reason why men philosophize is that most of them want to discover or create truths which are absolutely and universally true. They have been taught by religious thinkers that it is possible to achieve such truths, and, even when they reject religious truth-claims, they still want to arrive at conclusions which seem to be absolute and universal. Scientific reasoning cannot yield such conclusions.

Many men want to arrive at conclusions which are absolute and therefore permanent because they do not like to change their ideas and/or because they fear continual social reform. If all truths are temporary and imperfect, we must strive continually to improve them. Few people enjoy believing that such continuous intellectual work is necessary. Moreover, if old truths are constantly being replaced by new and more reliable truths, men ought to reform both their personal rules of conduct and their state constitutions and laws continuously. Many conservatives dislike and fear such changes.

Finally, some men philosophize partly because they are paid to do so. The knowledge that one can earn a living by teaching philosophy influences students of philosophy. In recent years, of course, a few teaching positions have been given to those who believe and teach that philosophy is nonsense, but the number of teaching positions in philosophy departments available to men who will teach that some philosophy makes sense is many times as large. It is difficult to teach what one does not believe, and it is easy to learn to believe what one will be paid to teach. Men like to feel useful and important, and they can feel neither when teaching something they consider meaningless.

It is true, of course, that some able men study and accept scientific ideas partly in order to earn money by teaching them. But no universities require that scientists be positivists. Scientists are only required to accept the doctrines and methodology of their own usually narrow scientific specialty. When thinking about other subjects, they are not only allowed, but in fact encouraged to be mormons, baptists, theosophists, spiritualists, idealists, etc. Hence it does not pay to be a positivist in the same way it pays, in job offers and promotions, to be religious or philosophic or both.

Most philosophic ideas are senseless, but, paradoxically, they usually continue to be accepted, partly because they are meaningless, long after meaningful but false ideas equally old have been abandoned. Acceptance of a meaningful idea has practical consequences which are pleasant or painful. A meaningless idea has no such consequences. It does not matter whether it is true or false. Hence, it may be retained indefinitely.

To illustrate this point, let us assume that a man believes (1) that all toadstools are edible and (2) that all toadstools are ideal rather than material. The first belief has practical consequences. It will lead to eating poisonous toadstools, and the unpleasant results may cause the eater to change his idea about toadstools. The second belief is meaningless and has no practical results. Hence, the believer will never have any direct, obvious reason for abandoning it, and he may honor this belief because he was taught it as a child by his mother.

E. Why Philosophers Sometimes Seem to Agree

Like theologians, philosophers cannot determine who is right when they disagree, and they usually disagree. Competing and conflicting systems of philosophy are incredibly numerous and various. Nevertheless, some philosophers do seem to agree on certain conclusions. How can this be explained?

To begin with, different philosophers often want to believe the same non-ethical religious dogmas, especially those of natural religion. As we have noted, philosophy largely consists of desired religious conclusions and the philosophic arguments used to support them.

Secondly, different philosophers may wish to support and believe the same social or political theories, especially those which have been localy popular in recent years. For instance, they may want to believe that a monarchical constitution is superior to a republican one, or *vice versa*. Hence, some philosophers have agreed that men have a natural right to elect their rulers, and others have agreed that kings have a divine right to rule their countries.

Thirdly, most philosophers have wanted to support traditional rules of conduct, such as the rules that one should not steal, murder, lie, etc. If they had not tried to justify these rules, they would not have been financially supported or even tolerated by other men.

Fourth, most philosophers have always wished to support political and economic rulers against rebellious subjects, partly because they themselves are personally members of the dominant classes and partly because those who support these rulers are usually rewarded for doing so and punished for not doing so.

Finally, philosophers often appear to agree when they do not because they use the same words to describe different things. For instance, if ten philosophers agree that "reality is ideal," this does not prove that they really agree. One philosopher may use the term *ideal* as a synonym for *spiritual*, another for *mental*, another for *personal*, and still another for *conscious*.

The general conclusion is that philosophers do not always agree when they seem to agree, and that when they do agree this does not imply that they are able to determine philosophically what is true. Rather, when they agree, they usually do so because they have non-philosophic reasons for wanting to arrive at the same conclusion.

F. The Harmful Effects of Philosophy

We turn now to the effects of philosophic thinking upon human activities. We are convinced that such thinking has seriously harmful effects for various reasons.

In the first place, most philosophy has been developed and used as an apology for whatever religious creed happens to be conventional at the time. Plato and Aristotle were deeply concerned with the preservation of faith in the gods of Olympus, and in the associated moral ideas. They called the critics of such ideas "sophists," not because these critics were illogical but because they were radical, and the word *sophist* has remained an epithet ever since. The efforts of Christian philosophers to support Christianity are well known. Since philosophy has usually been developed and taught in order to support existing religious beliefs, it has all of the harmful effects ascribed to religion in the previous chapter.

Even when philosophy is not religious, it has some of the harmful effects of religious philosophy because philosophic and religious thinking resemble each other. Both are deductive, yield absolute conclusions, and cause men to disagree widely and continuously. As a result, non-religious philosophers also tend to become dogmatic, arrogant, obscurantist, and jesuitical. Men who are certain they alone know what is absolutely good, true, and beautiful are remarkably conceited. Because they are sure they are right, they find it easy to rationalize the use of bad logic and/or brutal measures to defend their conclusions.

Moreover, the reason upon which philosophers claim to rely is a personal reason. Since their conclusions are unverified personal opinions based upon such a personal reason, they regard criticism of these conclusions as criticism of themselves. The scientist can refer critics and doubters to his observations and experiments, but the philosopher can refer them only to his arguments, which are inevitably personal and dogmatic. Hence the philosopher is much more likely than the scientist to take criticism personally and emotionally.

The most harmful effect of contemporary nonreligious philosophy is that it prejudices many promising students and the public at large against scientific ideas. If truth can be discovered by rational deduction from innate ideas in an armchair, why should men observe the world or perform laborious experiments? If philosophic truth is absolutely certain, the probable truths of science are clearly inferior. If the world is unreal, why bother to study it? If scientific facts about "material" reality are inferior to philosophic truths about "spiritual" reality, surely the most able students should devote their time to the latter. If philosophers can solve problems of personal or "moral" conduct, and scientists cannot, we should listen to the former more than to the later. Since resources are limited, every belief that causes us to devote labor and money to religion and philosophy tends to reduce the labor and money devoted to science.

The teaching of philosophy not only reduces the amount of resources devoted to science but seriously handicaps scientific researchers because it induces them to take philosophic ideas into the observatory or laboratory with them. Philosophic dogmas about perfect motion, perfect forms, moral conduct, metaphysical causation, freedom of the will, ultimate reality, absolute space and time, etc., have often prevented scientists from conceiving fruitful hypotheses or means of checking existing hypotheses and have often distorted scientific observation. Perhaps what scientists need most today is to free themselves from philosophic ideas. Einstein is supposed to have freed science of the concepts of absolute time and space, but he still believed that science reveals only "an infinitesimal part of the *intelligence* manifested in nature." Such metaphysical concepts are a serious obstacle to scientific progress.

Philosophers reduce public support for scientific research not only by persuading some people that philosophers alone can deal with the most profound and important human problems but also by persuading other people that philosophy is useless and/or nonsensical. When the average practical man becomes dimly aware that philosophic or religious theorists are talking nonsense, he often concludes that all theory, scientific as well as philosophic, is useless. This is perhaps the chief reason why so many Americans distrust and dislike theorists and university professors. To persuade men to respect sound academic theorists, we must teach both laymen and professors to distinguish between sense and nonsense, between science and non-science.

"If these [scientific] ideas be destined, as I believe they are, to be more and more firmly established . . . ; if that scientific spirit be fated, as I believe it is, to extend itself into all departments of human thought, and to become coextensive with the range of knowledge; if . . . it discovers, as I believe it will, that there is but one kind of knowledge and but one method of acquiring it; then we . . . may justly feel it our highest duty to recognize the advisableness of improving our natural knowledge. . . ."

T. H. Huxley, *On the Advisableness of Improving Natural Knowledge* (1866)

"Force, gravity, attraction, and words of this sort, are serviceable for reasonings and computations concerning motion and bodies in motion, but not for understanding the simple nature of motion itself, or for denoting so many distinct qualities. Certainly, as far as regards attraction, it is clear that it is adopted by Newton, not as a real, physical quality, but merely as a mathematical hypothesis."

George Berkeley, *De Motu* (1710)

CHAPTER IV. SCIENCE

WE HAVE EXAMINED two classes of truth-claims, the religious and the philosophic. In this chapter we turn to the third and last basic class, those which constitute science or the sciences.

Philosophy has been called the mother of the sciences. All sciences were long considered a part of philosophy and therefore the pioneer creators of each science called themselves philosophers. This history suggests that philosophy and science have a great deal in common, and that the individual sciences were separated from philosophy only because they grew larger and more important. In fact, however, science differs radically from philosophy.

Each individual science began, grew, and prospered only when and because some men ceased to reason religiously and/or philosophically and began to reason scientifically about its problems. In the beginning, and indeed until recently, these men called themselves philosophers but they created the new sciences only by becoming scientists in practice if not in name. Today we call nearly all of them scientists. They have now extended their investigation to cover all classes of human problems. Nothing it left for philosophers to do except to discuss the meaningless questions to which scientific methods cannot be applied.

A. Definition of Science

Comte used the terms *positive* and *positive science* to describe the theories which we include in science. From this is derived the name of his general doctrine, *positivism*. Apparently the term *positive* was then used to distinguish real science from pseudosciences like astrology and theology. In the century since Comte's death, the unqualified term *science* has come to mean what Comte meant by positive science.

The bare word *science* may refer to scientific institutions, equipment, activities, etc., as well as to scientific theories. We shall use it to refer solely to scientific theories.

1. *Science Includes All Truth-Claims Created by Scientific Reasoning*

At noted before, we define religion, philosophy, and science as the products respectively of religious, philosophic, and scientific reasoning. Thus science includes all theories created by the use of scientific methods of research. We shall define such methods broadly so that science can include all factual truths. As Karl Pearson noted some sixty years ago,

> The field of science is unlimited; its material is endless, every group of natural phenomena, every phase of social life, every stage of past or present development is material for science. *The unity of all science consists alone in its method, not in its material.* (*The Grammar of Science*, 1937 ed., page 16)

It is often said that science includes only general theories and excludes the facts on which these theories are based.

This distinction seems unwise. It is frequently hard to distinguish between a bare fact and a theory. Thus most visual perception includes unconscious theorizing or interpretation of sensations. Moreover, the problem of how to obtain or verify facts is often very difficult. Therefore, we prefer to say that science includes both facts and theories. Indeed, we have used the term *theory* to cover both facts and theories throughout this book.

It may be worth noting that all scientific theories are verbal statements. Hence, they are created, not discovered. Men can discover things, but they create statements about them.

We wish to emphasize that science includes its presuppositions or basic principles, its definitions, and all verified theories as to how one scientific fact or principle is related to another. Some philosophers have claimed these theories for philosophy (see p. 92 above).

The so-called presuppositions of science are meaningless unless they are verifiable in theory and useless unless they are verifiable in practice. But any verified theory is a scientific truth. The same reasoning applies to theories as to how scientific truths are related to each other. As for definitions, they are all old or new. The former can be found in dictionaries and the latter should be formulated by those who plan to use them. Hence, scientists should create and elaborate their own definitions, presuppositions, and theories as to how different scientific principles are related. There is no good reason for philosophers to do this.

It is often claimed that all definitions are arbitrary and hence cannot be true or false. Thus *black* may be redefined to mean what *white* now means, and neither definition need be true or false. It may seem therefore that definitions are not a part of science (verified truth-claims). However, a complete scientific definition begins with a clause like "It is useful to define." Hence, it is verifiable. On the other hand, the remainder of the definition, the only part usually stated, is not a truth and does not imply any truths by definition.

2. *Naive and Sophisticated Science*

The term *science* is usually restricted to the ideas and activities of men who have consciously and systematically used a scientific method to gain new knowledge. But practical men had created a vast number of demonstrable factual theories useful in the arts and crafts long before systematic scientific research began. Since science includes all verified theories, it includes all the practical rules developed by artisans, farmers, rulers, etc., before and since the rise of modern scientific research as well as the results of such research.

Although the distinction between these two classes of scientific truths is widely recognized, there are no generally accepted names for them. We shall call them *naive* and *sophisticated science,* but shall often drop the qualifying adjective in speaking of sophisticated science.

We include under sophisticated science the facts and theories created by practical inventors like Edison and the Wright Brothers and by development engineers as well as those created by highly educated scientists engaged in pure research. All such men are conscious specialized creators of true scientific theories. Our distinction between naive and sophisticated science is not identical with or closely related to the distinction between applied and pure science. It is a distinction based upon the experience and methods of the person creating knowledge. However, naive science consists largely, perhaps entirely, of applied science, while sophisticated science includes a large amount of applied science and nearly all pure science.

Naive science includes the useful verified conclusions arrived at by contemporary men untrained in and not engaged in scientific research as well as those of primitive man. When a housewife undertakes to find out why her vacuum cleaner has suddenly ceased to run, she may form the hypothesis that the electric fuse has blown and test it by plugging in her machine on another circuit. The resulting conclusion is a part of naive science. It is based upon observation and experiment, is verifiable by other observers, and is thus radically different from religion and philosophy. All the trivial but sound conclusions made daily by practical men are a part of naive science.

Virtually all accumulated knowledge up to the year 1800 was naive science, and a very large part of present knowledge is naive science. Sophisticated science is almost entirely the product of a small number of western inventors, engineers, and scientists who began to use planned observation and experiments to advance science about 400 years ago.

As we have explained before, there are many objections to Comte's theory that ideas on all subjects go through his three stages of development successively. Perhaps the most serious is that it implies that men had no scientific ideas until fairly recently. Since they undoubtedly knew enough to become highly civilized, his theory suggests that theological and metaphysical ideas alone are sufficient to achieve this. Our distinction between naive and sophisticated science permits us to save must of Comte's theory of intellectual evolution by restricting it to pure (non-technological) theory and substituting *sophisticated science* for *positive science* as the third stage.

It is customary to distinguish sharply between science and art, but this can be very misleading. Theories cannot be divided into two classes, those which belong to science and those which belong to art. All meaningful theories are scientific hypotheses or truths regardless of whether they deal with artistic or other problems.

The term *art* has several quite different senses. It may refer to the theory of one or more vocations, in which case it is a part of applied science. It may refer to works of art or the labor which creates them, in which case it is neither a part of science nor of any other body of theory. And aesthetics, a part of philosophy, is sometimes called the theory of art. But there is no sense in which *art* designates a body of theory outside religion and philosophy which should be distinguished from science.

Those who restrict the word *science* to what we called sophisticated science sometimes use the term *common sense* to describe either a method of achieving truth different from scientific methods or the ideas achieved by a different method, but this term is ambiguous. Those who use it rarely define it precisely. They often argue that religious and philosophic ideas are a result of common sense. Nevertheless, *common sense* can be used as a synonym for *naive science.* When so used, it can not include any non-scientific or anti-scientific ideas. This definition of *common sense* is implicit in the old definition of science as *organized common sense.*

3. *Science Includes Logic and Mathematics*

Logic has long been treated as a subdivision of philosophy In the previous chapter, we explained why we believe this is wrong. Both logic and mathematics are a part of science.

Science includes the theory of how to reason scientifically. To reason thus, one must use inductive and deductive logic and mathematics. Inductive logic is the most important, and has therefore often been called the theory of scientific method. But deductive logic and mathematics are very useful to scientists. The fact that deductive logic has also been commonly used by theologians and philosophers does not imply that it belongs to religion or philosophy. If it were not useful to scientists, it should be abandoned. Since it is useful to them, and since they alone can create truths, deductive logic is a part of scientific methodology and, hence, a part of science.

Some positivists have asserted or implied that both deductive logic and mathematics are systems of arbitrary axioms and formally valid inferences from these axioms and therefore cannot belong to science, a system of factual truths. We agree fully that arbitrary axioms and inferences from them are not a part of science. However, the theory of how to state or choose useful axioms and the theory of how to infer useful conclusions from such axioms is verifiable, and when verified becomes a part of science, specifically a part of the theory of scientific methodology.

For us, deductive logic is the theory of how to formulate useful deductive syllogisms, not these syllogisms themselves, and mathematics is the theory of how to formulate useful mathematical demonstrations. Hence, logic and mathematics do not include meaningless logical and mathematical propositions.

4. *Scientific Explanation*

It is sometimes asserted that scientists do not explain "why" things happen but only "how" they happen. In *Science and the Modern World* (1925), A. N. Whitehead remarked that Galileo and his theological critics "were at hopeless cross purposes . . . Galileo keeps harping on how things happen, whereas his adversaries had a complete theory as to why things happen" (p. 9). This simple distinction between how and why is misleading. The question "why?" may be meaningless or meaningful. Priests and philosophers have often asked the question "why?" in a meaningless way and have given a meaningless answer, as did the priests who criticized Galileo. It is possible, however, to ask the question "why?" meaningfully and give a meaningful answer.

To illustrate this point, let us consider two cases. The first is that of a woman whose diamond brooch has disappeared and who wants to know how and/or why it has disappeared. Both questions could be answered by a descripition of how it had fallen from her dress and been lost in her garden. A full description would include all the facts which might answer the question "why?" when *why* is used in a meaningful way. However, it is always possible to use *why* in a religious or philosophic sense, in which case it is meaningless. The so-called problem of causation, "why does a cause always have the same effect?" illustrates this nonsensical use of the term *why*. This question does not suggest any hypotheses which might be tested. It is, therefore, a senseless question.

Other writers have tried to distinguish between scientific and religious or philosophic thinking by saying that science is descriptive and the latter are explanatory. This closely resembles the distinction between the question "how?" and the question "why?" and is misleading for much the same reason. An explanation may be religious, philosophic, or scientific. Scientists do not offer religious or philosophic explanations but they do offer scientific explanations. A scientific explanation merely describes the conditions and causes, but no other meaningful and useful explanation of anything is possible. The term *explain* is often used in this scientific sense by laymen as well as by scientists.

5. *Scientific Theories are Means to Ends*

The true theories which constitute science are means to ends. Men create truths in order to do what they previously wanted to do. They rarely, if ever, create them in order to enjoy them directly.

It is true, of course, that mental exercise may be as pleasant as physical exercise, and therefore an end-in-itself, but mental exercise is not truth. It may be enjoyed in bridge or chess far more easily than in original scientific research. And it is the exercise, not the true theory incidentally created, which is usually pleasant.

Many religious and philosophic theories have been created and accepted because men want to believe them. But these theories are meaningless or false. They are not pleasant truths.

Some scientific truths also are pleasant to believe. For instance, a public opinion survey may show that our city is widely admired. But the vast majority of truths are useful only as means for doing things we want to do. And those which are directly gratifying are also useful as means to other ends. Moreover, we should be especially sceptical of truth-claims which are pleasant because it is so easy to believe what we want to believe.

It has been argued that scientific truth is an end-in-itself because men enjoy contemplating truth. But many truths, such as statements concerning the melting points of metals, are very dull and obviously bore 999 out of 1000 people. And interesting truths, such as those concerning the history of man, are no more interesting than the legends and myths accepted before these truths were known.

The phrase, *contemplating truth* is very vague if not meaningless. Do we contemplate truth when we read a vivid history rapidly? Or must we concentrate for a considerable time on a single sentence? And do not religious and philosophic thinkers claim to enjoy contemplating dogmas which we have shown to be meaningless?

When scientists solve a problem, they have a feeling of accomplishment which may be associated and confused with the sensation of thinking over or "contemplating" the results of their research. And other men may enjoy learning of and "contemplating" these results if they understand them and find them flattering or useful. But few if any men enjoy the pure contemplation of truths which are neither flattering nor useful.

The conflict between religion and science has been called a conflict between emotion and reason, between the heart and the mind. We believe that this is misleading as well as meaningless. However men reason—whether religiously, philosophically, or scientifically—they do so in order to achieve desired and usually pleasant results. When they reason religiously or philosophically, they usually reach conclusions which are pleasant because they are directly satisfying, but they also hope in vain that these conclusions will be useful. When they reason scientifically, they achieve some conclusions which are directly satisfying and some which are not. But all scientific conclusions are actually or potentially useful, i.e., indirectly satisfying. Thus, on the whole and in the long run, scientific thinking is far more emotionally satisfying than religious or philosophic thinking. The thinking itself is less emotional, but the results are much more pleasant emotionally.

We are assuming, of course, that scientific thinking is productive. Before men learned enough about scientific thinking to make it yield results in difficult cases, religious and philosophic thinking was more satisfying. Even today it may be temporarily more satisfying in dealing with problems which scientists are still unable to solve. But whenever scientific thinking is productive, it is more emotionally satisfying than any other thinking.

B. Scientific Methods

It is customary to speak of *the* scientific method, but this is a phrase which has no referent. There are various scientific methods, which can be exhibited, but there is no single abstract scientific method. Therefore, we speak of scientific methods, not of *the* scientific method.

We have defined scientific truths as those which are created by using scientific methods. It is essential, therefore, that we explain what makes a method scientific. The following explanation of such methods is not intended as a guide for working scientists but as an explanation for intelligent laymen of how these methods differ from religious and philosophic methods of creating truth-claims.

Scientific methods of creating true theories differ radically from religious and philosophic methods. In explaining how they differ, we shall emphasize two points: (1) the scientist assumes that every event is determined or caused, and (2) scientific methods are empirical, i.e., they always include, and usually begin with, observation.

1. *Scientists Accept Determinism*

Determinism, the theory that all events are caused or determined, is the basic working principle of scientists. A cause is a preceding event which determines a subsequent event. If events did not have causes, it would be impossible to discover why they happen and hence impossible to learn how to control them. In other words, scientific reasoning would be useless.

The principle of causality or determinism is usually stated briefly as the rule that every event has one or more causes. However, this theory is unverified. No method of determining whether any event is uncaused can be conceived. The most that can be proven is that the cause is unknown.

To avoid this criticism, Arthur Pap has suggested that the principle of causality be restated as an optative sentence: "Would that everything could be predicted and explained!" However, this is mere wishful thinking. All scientific principles should be factual and verifiable.

We suggest that the principle of causation should be restated as the rule that in scientific research it usually pays to assume that the events being studied are caused and that it never pays to assume the opposite. This version of the principle can be, in fact has been, verified by experience.

While older versions of the principle are imperfect, they have been extraordinarily useful to scientists. The revision which we have suggested would affect the behavior of scientists little, if any, because they have nearly always acted as if they were applying it.

The theory that it pays to assume that every event is caused is entirely different from the meaningless philosophic doctrine that nature is orderly. The scientist recognizes that events are often disorderly. He believes that both disorderly and orderly events are determined and he has often been able to discover how both kinds of events are caused. The fact that an event is determined does not mean it is orderly or rational or anything else, unless these adjectives are arbitrarily defined as synonyms of *caused*.

Some critics of determinism have claimed that it implies that men cannot influence events. This is a gross error. Human acts are events which influence other events. When properly planned on the basis of applied science, they often cause desired results. Determinism does imply that human acts are determined. But, if they were not, it would be impossible for parents to train children and for psychologists to study human behavior scientifically. We shall discuss these points again (pp. 208-12).

2. *Scientists Rely on Observation*

Religion is based upon revelation, philosophy upon reason, and science upon observation. Instead of reading a holy book or examining his own preconceptions, the scientist begins by observing events about and within him. Instead of starting with religious or philosophic dogmas, he begins with individual observations. After reflecting upon what he has observed, he tries to formulate generalizations which explain and/or describe the observed objects and events. These tentative generalizations are called hypotheses. They are verifiable but as yet unverified ideas. They can be verified only by further observation, which must include observations by other scientists. When several competent scientists have made observations which confirm a new hypothesis, it is usually accepted as a new scientific truth.

An accepted scientific truth may be made questionable at any time by further observations which seem to contradict it. No scientific theory is complete, perfect, or absolutely true. Unlike the products of revelation and reason, such theories are obviously the creation of fallible men using methods which are constantly yielding more accurate and more numerous observations and conclusions. The history of science is largely the history of the correction and elaboration of previously accepted scientific truths.

We have said that scientific methods are empirical. Some scientists use the adjective *empirical* to describe experiments which are not guided by specific hypotheses. For example, J. B. Conant refers repeatedly to "cut-and-try or empirical experimentation." We have used *empirical* quite differently, i.e., to describe theories based on observation. In this more usual sense, all scientific methods and conclusions are empirical. In Conant's sense, naive science is empirical, but most sophisticated science is non-empirical. However, able scientists still use "cut-and-try" research methods on some problems, such as the search for antibiotic drugs, because they have no working hypothesis which suggests better-planned research.

Scientific observation must be unbiased and adequate. Many men have searched for and found evidence to support a desired conclusion and have ignored other conflicting evidence. In some schools—such as those of law, religion, and advertising—men are carefully trained to misuse evidence in this way.

Moreover, unbiased men often fail to reach correct scientific conclusions because they do not make enough observations. They draw conclusions from too few cases, often because they are untrained in statistics. Some unbiased observers who observe enough cases do not select their cases properly. They get a sample which is large enough but is not typical of the statistical universe they are studying.

In its most general sense, *observation* includes what one reads about the observations of other scientists. Perhaps the greatest aid to the formulation of fruitful new hypotheses, especially those needed to guide further personal observation, is a review of the written reports of previous students of the problem in question.

a. Scientific Reports

Scientific research requires not only unbiased and adequate observation but accurate, meaningful, and objective verbal reports of what has been observed.

To make accurate reports, the scientist must usually be able to measure. The history of modern science is in large part a history of the development of measurement and of measuring instruments such as the clock, the thermometer, and the barometer. This is so generally recognized that it requires no elaboration here.

To make accurate reports, one should report only the bare facts that have been observed. This may sound obvious, but many would-be scientific observers have reported seeing witches, ghosts, miracles, flying saucers, etc. They have failed to distinguish between what has been observed and what has been inferred from the observation. The mystic who reports direct communion with the spirit of the universe, for instance, is not reporting his observation but his biased personal interpretation of it. A scientific hypothesis to explain it cannot be formulated until many men have accurately reported the crude observations or experiences upon which such mystical interpretations are based. History shows that it is very difficult to learn to distinguish between experience and interpretation, especially when certain kinds of interpretations have long been customary.

Scientific reports are verbal reports. To make them as clear and accurate as possible, the reporter should apply the semantic rules stated in the introduction to this book. We shall review them very briefly here.

Perhaps the basic idea of semantics is that verbal reports function like maps. They describe what has been observed. Many of the rules which apply to map-making also apply to report-writing. There should be no symbols on a map which do not refer to some feature of the mapped area, and there should be no words in an affirmative scientific report which do not refer to or describe some observed thing. Except when they deny that something has been observed, scientific reports should include only nouns which name observed things or events, adjectives and adverbs which qualify things or events, verbs which describe observed events or relate nouns to adjectives, prepositions which indicate how things and events are related, etc. The rule that basic nouns should denote observed things or events is the one which is most often violated and with the most harmful results.

Scientific reports should be as objective and uncolored as possible. All meaningful words connote as well as denote or describe, but scientists should use those which connote the least. This is especially important for social scientists since they deal with problems about which men are most apt to be biased.

Instead of reporting that a person "sneaked into" a room, the scientist says that he "entered quietly." He refers to a black man as a "negro," not as a "niger." He does so in order to be objective, not in order to be courteous.

Every word is more or less loaded, and some highly loaded terms like *democracy, dictatorship, capitalism,* and *socialism* have no relatively neutral synonyms. New words may be invented but they soon become associated with the same emotions and become almost equally loaded. Moreover, it is usually confusing to invent new terms. Hence, it is often proper to use highly loaded terms. When they are used, the user should define them in neutral terms, if possible, and should warn his readers that they are loaded.

Like maps, scientific reports contain only pertinent facts about what has been observed. They fail to give information deemed irrelevant or unimportant. The selection of relevant facts is guided by a theory as to how the maps or reports are to be used. For other uses, different maps and reports of the same areas and events may be needed. No set of maps or reports can give all possible information about what has been observed.

b. Scientific Hypotheses

We have explained why reports of scientific observations should be unambiguous and meaningful. It is equally important that hypotheses should be unambiguous and meaningful. To formulate a meaningful hypothesis, one must conceive of some method of verification. To formulate a useful hypothesis, one must go further and conceive a practical method of verification. In other words, one must be able to specify in detail the feasible observations which would prove or disprove the theory. The solution of the problem of verification cannot be an afterthought. An alleged hypothesis is meaningless, and therefore not an hypothesis, until the words in it have been made meaningful by explaining how it can be verified. The act of formulating a hypothesis can be separated from the act of verification, but not from the act of conceiving a method of verification. Therefore, when trying to formulate hypotheses, scientists should strive to conceive simultaneously a method of verification.

To create an hypothesis which suggests the same method of verification to different scientists, and is therefore, meaningful, one must use meaningful words only. All of the semantic rules stated in our introduction apply. Nouns must have referents, verbs must describe observable events, and all other words must further specify what is to be observed in order to verify the hypothesis.

Hypotheses are sometimes said to be intuitive. Certainly, observation alone does not guarantee a fruitful hypothesis. Many men can observe forever without conceiving new hypotheses. Even among the most gifted thinkers, new and fruitful hypotheses are rare and gratifying achievements. Sometimes, moreover, these achievements occur in idle moments, for instance when one is lying awake at night, long after observation and systematic reflection has ceased. At such times, a hypothesis may seem to be unrelated to observation, but this is an illusion. Like all other events, ideas have necessary conditions and causes. Meaningful hypotheses must be based upon observation because they consist entirely of words which report past observations and predict future observation. Some men react more quickly and/or completely to observations than other men do, but this does not prove that their hypotheses are intuitive. Indeed, *intuitive* is a meaningless word, for it is impossible to conceive and agree upon a method of proving that any idea is intuitive.

In recent years a few writers—including Popper and Wisdom—have argued that all scientific observors have or formulate hypotheses before they observe or experiment and that, therefore, there is no such thing as an inductive method. They call the methods of scientists *hypothetico-deductive.* Even if their claim is true, which we doubt, the question of whether scientists create hypotheses before they observe or *vice versa* is trivial. It resembles the old question of whether the egg or the chicken appears first. The important question is quite different. It is whether observation or deduction verifies conclusions. In religious and philosophic reasoning, deduction proves that conclusions are true. In scientific reasoning it merely suggests conclusions which can be tested by observation. Since scientific reasoning relies finally on observation rather than deduction, we believe that it should be called inductive rather than deductive even when it includes deduction.

3. *Scientific Methods and Positivism*

We have devoted only a few pages explicity to scientific methods, but the entire theory of logical positivism, to which this book is largely devoted, is but one part of the general theory of scientific methods. The main thesis of positivism is that men can create truths by using scientific methods but not by using religious or philosophic methods of truth seeking. The general theory of scientific methods includes an explanation of why they alone yield verifiable or meaningful truths. Hence, positivism is a part of scientific methodology, and this book is merely a statement of part of the theory of scientific methods. Positivism is not a philosophy or a part of logic but a statement of the reasons why men should use only scientific methods of truth creation.

C. Some Criticisms of Science and Positivism

1. *The Alleged Limitations of Science*

Those who wish to restrict the application of scientific methods to the so-called "natural" sciences often argue that these methods have certain "limitations" which make them unsuitable for use in studies dealing with personal and social behavior. The very term *natural sciences* itself implies this because it suggests that other sciences deal with events which are not natural and therefore not subject to prediction. This idea was common among scientists as well as priests until very recently.

The argument that scientific methods are only applicable to certain problems was elaborated by J. W. N. Sullivan in a widely read book, *The Limitations of Science* (1933). He repeated many of the anti-scientific arguments now popular among the more intellectual supporters of religion and philosophy. We shall therefore summarize and answer his main points.

Sullivan began his attack upon science by asserting that, "One of the least disputable laws of physical science states the universe is steadily running down" (p. 24). This implies that "at some particular moment in the past, a perfectly organized universe sprang suddenly into being." This conclusion is so startling that "we cannot believe it is the whole truth." Hence, scientific method is limited or defective.

This reasoning is unsound. The theory that the universe is running down was never more than a stimulating hypothesis, if indeed it was ever meaningful, and it had been ably criticized if not refuted before Sullivan used it in 1933 to prove that science has limitations. Indeed, Sullivan himself noted some evidence that matter is being created in space. More important, the fact that the universe is running down would not prove that it had once sprung suddenly into being. It could easily run down forever. And the idea of springing suddenly into being is unverifiable and senseless. Finally, if this inference were valid, meaningful, and partly verified, the mere fact that it is startling to some men would not justify the conclusion that science is limited.

A second alleged limitation of science, according to Sullivan, is that it deals only with the "*quantitative* aspects" of our experience. It ignores many other elements of our experience, such as "our perceptions of colour, etc., our response to beauty, our sense of mystic communion with God . . ."

(p. 133). This argument is invalid because numerous reports of quantitative scientific research on our perceptions of color, beauty, etc., are available. In fact, every human sensation can be studied quantitatively. This does not mean we have already developed ideal methods of quantitative research on human sensations, but we have made progress and there is nothing to prevent further progress. Moreover, there are many verified non-quantitative theories in science, such as the theories of biological, geological, and social evolution.

In elaborating his second alleged limitation, Sullivan claimed modern science holds "that the primary qualities [size, shape, weight] alone are real—the others [color, sound, etc.] are in some sense illusory." Thus science reduces "the real to colourless, soundless odourless bodies in motion . . ." (pp. 131-2). This claim is partly nonsensical, partly false, and partly ambiguous.

The noun *quality* is meaningless. Men observe qualified objects, not qualities, and these objects cannot be classified into primary and secondary objects. To say that objects qualified in certain ways "are in some sense illusory" is either meaningless, because unverifiable, or a tautology.

Moreover, demonstrably illusory objects are qualified in every way, i.e., by primary as well as secondary "qualities." Hence, all "qualities" are often illusory in this sense. Conversely, when objects are demonstrably observed, it is misleading to say that they are partly real and partly illusory.

These terms, *real* and *illusory*, can be either meaningful or meaningless. Philosophers use them in a metaphysical sense, scientists in a scientific sense. That is why philosophers, and scientists influenced by philosophers, often seem to be talking sense when they are in fact talking nonsense. The test is whether one can imagine a method of verifying the statement in question. Thus one can prove that a ghost seen by one man was not seen by other men, and is therefore illusory or unreal, but one cannot prove that a red ball is illusory or that a colorless ball is real.

There is a closely related error, popularized by Eddington, that the world revealed by atomic physics is not only different from but inconsistent with that revealed by our sensations. Actually, one supplements the other and there is no conflict between them. The fact that sensations are due to molecular movements does not prove our sensations are non-existent or misleading. All discoveries concerning atomic and molecular movements have been made by means of human sensations. These discoveries constitute additional information about the observable world, but they are no more true or real than the sensations upon which they are based. Thus modern science does not undermine or invalidate the sense data upon which 19th century scientific materialism was based.

The third major limitation of science claimed by Sullivan is its assumption of determinism. We have already discussed this assumption once (pp. 135-36) and shall discuss it again (pp. 208-12). The assumption of determinism is essential to all intelligent search for explanations. Events can only be explained if they have causes.

It is, of course, obvious that the scientific methods used today are limited in the sense that they can be improved. At times Sullivan falls back upon this truism to support his attack upon science, but this is not his chief thesis. It would scarcely be necessary to write a book to prove that present methods of scientific research can be improved.

To Sullivan and his like, scientific methods seem extremely limited because they cannot be used to support what they wish to believe, their religion or philosophy. This is the great limitation of scientific thought for them! They conclude that since scientific method is severely limited, the method of religion and/or philosophy is not. It would be equally logical to argue that since American doctors cannot cure leprosy, African witch doctors may be able to do so.

In his lucid and often brilliant book, *The Scientific Outlook* (1931), Bertrand Russell asserted that scientific method is limited in three ways: (1) scientists are unable to prove that induction is valid, (2) they cannot prove that an unexperienced ultimate reality exists, and (3) scientific theories are abstract and give less information than they appear to (pp. 74-84).

These objections are unjustified. We have already explained why the philosophic problems of whether induction is valid and whether ultimate reality exists are senseless, (pp. 96-97, 110-11). As for his third point, scientific theories are abstract because all words are abstract. Since all factual reasoning is verbal, it is all abstract, but we cannot see why this limits scientific reasoning. Indeed, it seems to us that it is only because factual reasoning is abstract that those who use it are able to create verifiable and useful theories. Russell did not suggest any other method of reasoning which would yield such theories, and we cannot conceive of any. Hence, his third "limitation of scientific method" seems as unsound as his first two.

2. *The Marxist Criticism of Positivism*

Maurice Cornforth, a British Marxist, has attacked positivism in two books and several articles. In his book, *In Defense of Philosophy* (1950), he charged that, "Positivism concentrates within itself all the most negative features of bourgeois philosophy—the doctrine of the limitations of knowledge and the unknowability of the real world" (p. iii). Positivists limited knowledge, he thinks, because they limit scientists to study of the observable world revealed by sense data and reject alleged knowledge of the real world. Actually, modern positivists do not set limits to scientific knowledge; rather they claim that many traditional questions, and all answers to them, are senseless. They do not say the real word is unknowable; they merely claim that the philosophic term, *real world*, is meaningless.

Cornforth has also charged that positivists interpret scientific knowledge as knowledge of sense-data rather than as knowledge of the objective world. It is true that positivists believe all knowledge is derived from experience, i.e., from sense-data, and that all true statements can be verified by sense-data. But this does not deny the objective world. Sense data result from contact with an objective world (see p. 97 above).

It is only when philosophers make unverifiable and meaningless statements about insensible metaphysical things that positivists protest. Verifiable statements about sensible things are not inconsistent with science or positivism. Whether objects and the objective world exist or merely appear to exist is a meaningless question. Whether they can be observed by different observers under given conditions is a scientific question, and positivists accept the findings of scientists on scientific questions.

In sum, Cornforth and other dialectical materialists who attack positivists as idealists have failed to grasp the positivist position and have taken seriously the meaningless philosophic problem of idealism versus realism.

3. *The Charge that Science is Cold or Inhuman*

Critics of science and positivism often assert that science is cold, lifeless or inhuman, thus implying that they prefer religion or philosophy because it is warm, alive, or human. This is a fine illustration of the way common words can be used in a sentence which seems to be meaningful but is actually meaningless. Science is not a thing which can be cold or warm. It is best defined as a body of statements and it is literally nonsensical to say that any statement is cold or warm, lifeless or alive, human or inhuman. It may be replied that neither the noun *science* nor these adjectives are being used literally, but in this case the statement becomes highly ambiguous. There are many ways in which any such statement can be interpreted symbolically, and a statement with many possible meanings is as confusing as a meaningless statement.

If *science* be interpreted to mean scientific activities, the same analysis applies. An activity cannot be cold or warm. *Inhuman* and *human* can be meaningfully applied to activities, but they are ambiguous. If we could agree upon reasonable definitions, we should find that some scientific activities are human and others are inhuman. The same is true, of course, of religious activities. Most men now realize that burning witches at the stake, a common religious activity at one time, was inhuman. Moreover, positivism does not claim that all scientific activities are human; it claims that truth can be created only by scientific methods, quite a different thing.

Critics of positivism sometimes charge that science is cold or inhuman because it ignores or denies the fact that men want to be emotionally satisfied. But nearly all scientific theories can now be used to help men do what they want to do, and it is always emotionally satisfying to do what one wants to do. While wishful thinking may be emotionally pleasant, the results of acting upon conclusions supported only by wishful thinking are often very unpleasant emotionally.

It is true that most positivists, like most philosophers and theologicians, are intellectuals. As such, they tend to praise intellectual activities too highly and to frown upon more sensual and emotional activities. But they have never pretended that revelation or rational intuition justifies this personal prejudice. Priests have usually taught that to be sensual is to be wicked, and philosophers have naively proclaimed that the life of reason is ethically supreme. Positivists, on the contrary, are convinced that there is no ethical basis for condemning sensual or emotional behavior. Indeed, they praise science as a means of providing emotional and sensual gratification. Thus they are far more human than philosophers and priests if human is defined as being sympathetic to normal human conduct.

Those who charge that science and/or positivism is cold and inhuman sometimes try to support this criticism by claiming that scientists and positivists ignore or oppose art, literature, music, and other things and activities which men enjoy emotionally. There are of course all kinds of scientists and positivists, and some may not enjoy or approve such things and activities, but there is nothing in scientific or positivistic theory opposed to art, literature, music, etc. Rather scientists and positivists strive to help men do whatever they want to do, and many men want to enjoy artistic objects and activities.

While positivists often enjoy literature and art, they do not believe that literary writers are as capable of creating new truths, or of choosing wisely among competing truth claims, as scientists. They believe that most literary writers have been trained to reason religiously or philosophically rather than scientifically. But, when they criticize literary works, they criticize the method of reasoning and the false conclusions. They do not condemn them because they are interesting, entertaining, or charming, but in spite of this. And they wholely approve of literary works which are truthful and instructive as well as charming.

Perhaps we should explain again (see p. 114 above) how science is related to works of art. Pure science is useful only when used to create applied science. Applied science helps men to produce the goods and services they want. All goods and services are more or less beautiful, i.e., artistically pleasing. All true theories as to how to make more beautiful goods are a part of applied science. They can be verified by experiments. Thus the traditional distinction between an art and an applied science is highly misleading.

D. How Science Benefits Men

We turn now to stress the vast benefits which have resulted from the use of scientific methods to create new truths. We noted that science is a means to an end, not an end-in-itself. As such, science, and science alone, helps men to decide what they most want to achieve and how to achieve it.

1. *Science Makes Men Healthier and Richer*

We could elaborate the vital point that science helps men do whatever they want to do by ennumerating the chief things that men want and explaining how science has helped men to achieve each of them more fully, but this seems unnecessary. For such elaboration we refer the reader to the numerous books on the application of science to human problems. However, we can suggest here how varied scientific achievements are by pointing out that today there are useful scientific books on how to select a wife, how to practice birth control, how to educate children, how to cure sick persons, how to treat the insane, how to decrease costs and increase output in every industry, how to entertain children and adults, how to make atom bombs, etc., etc. Scientists have dealt with almost every human problem, and have nearly always achieved some useful results.

It is easiest to demonstrate the great contributions of science when we have reasonably reliable statistics, notably with respect to population, sick persons, and industrial output. These subjects are closely related. The population of the world has doubled in the last 100 years because scientists have enabled men to reduce the death rate and to feed all of the additional population. In those nations where science is most advanced, population has doubled in the last 50 years and real wages have also risen sharply.

Economic progress, which causes an increase in population and/or a rise in real income, has been going on for thousands of years. But modern sophisticated science has brought about a notable increase in the rate of economic progress. Naive scientific thinking assured a slow rate of progress, but sophisticated scientific research has already caused a great speedup in progress and promises an even greater one for the future. Real wages in Europe and America have risen more in the last 100 years than in the previous 300 years, and are likely to rise more in the next 50 years than in the last 100, if there are no wars much more destructive than World Wars I and II. Continued birth control is of course essential to such progress, but birth control is a product of scientific research, not of religious or philosophic thinking, and such research will soon produce better and cheaper means of birth control.

The vast social gains achieved in recent centuries as a result of scientific thinking (both naive and sophisticated) can be best illustrated by comparing social statistics on Western Europe and North America, where scientific thinking is most common, with those on China or India, where sophisticated scientific thinking is new and rare. The birth and death rates are far higher, and literacy rate far lower, in China and India than in the United States. Most Asiatic peasants live in insect-ridden mud huts with little furniture and no glass in their windows. Most American farmers lives in clean houses with wooden floors, electricity, running water, telephone, and many other conveniences. It is in America that the results of modern scientific thinking are most apparent. American output per worker now increases about 2% a year. This means that the American real wages will probably increase by 200 to 300% in the next century. Such progress was unknown before the rise of modern science.

The effect of sophisticated science upon the growth of knowledge has been even greater than its effect upon real wages. Our knowledge has increased more in the last 300 years than in the previous 3000, and more in the last 100 years than in the previous 300. It will probably increase more in the next 50 years than in the last 100, and so on indefinitely.

2. *Science Makes Men Optimistic*

The whole idea of human progress is a positivist idea. It was developed by the chief precursors of positivism and/or pioneer positivists in the late 18th and early 19th centuries. Condorcet, the chief early proponent of the idea of progress, was a pioneer positivist. His contributions to positivism were highly valued by Comte, who himself further elaborated the idea of progress. Marx and Darwin, two other important contributors to this theory, were also strongly positivistic. The idea of progress was virtually unknown to religious and philosophic thinkers before 1800, and has been rejected by most of them since then. If the earth is meant to be a vale of tears, a period of moral trial before salvation and another life, why should men try to become more comfortable and happy now? Conversely, it is hard for men to long for heaven in the sky when they enjoy a sensible heaven on earth, and scientific progress promises such a heaven. To most philosophers who are not religious, the idea of progress is dubious because they have no means of reaching agreement on any conclusions and because they believe that "spiritual" things and ideal entities are far more important than "material" welfare. One of the best practical methods of detecting unscientific thinkers is to ask people their attitude toward progress. Those who deny or criticize or minimize progress are nearly always very critical of positivism.

Belief in progress is optimism. The growth of science has already converted most people in advanced countries from pessimism to optimism. The inevitable further spread of scientific thinking will make men optimistic in Asia and Africa as well as in Western Europe and North America. Theologians and philosophers will probably remain profoundly pessimistic, but their views will influence men less and less.

A theory of progress is meaningful only if it is verifiable. In other words, *progress* must be defined so that it can be measured.

Critics of theories of progress fall into two main classes. A few of them concede that progress must be verifiable and argue that the term *progress* should describe some other measureable events than the ones it is being used to describe. These critics often seem unaware that all definitions are arbitrary. But most critics claim that progress cannot be measured because it is a "spiritual" rather than a material thing. The effect of this argument, however, is to make the theory of progress meaningless, so that it becomes as absurd to say that progress has not occurred as to claim that it has.

3. *Science Makes Men More Peaceful*

One of the greatest gains due to scientific thinking is more peaceful agreement among men. In the past, men have agreed on social, political, moral, and similar issues almost entirely because of conquest, indoctrination, legal coercion, inquisition, economic pressure, social ostracism, etc. Scientific thinking now enables men to determine who is right and then agree peacefully on such issues.

For one interested in ideas, there is nothing more frustrating than the realization that there is no method of settling disputes over ideas. Young and naïve university graduates often believe that all human problems can be settled by sound reasoning. After numerous unsuccessful attempts to persuade other people to be reasonable, i.e., to accept their views, they gradually learn not only that most arguments over religion, politics, philosophy, ethics, etc., are useless but that they often turn friends into enemies. As the years pass, most educated men become more and more sceptical of all reasoning on non-vocational problems and less and less willing to engage in intellectual arguments. This is largely because religious and philosophic thinking are customary.

Science is based entirely upon observation and includes accepted methods of making, checking, and interpreting observations. When two scientists disagree, they have mutually agreed methods of settling their dispute peacefully. All that is necessary is to repeat the observations upon which the conflicting opinions are based. If no observations which would settle a meaningful dispute are practical, scientists agree that they do not know who is right. By contrast, priests and philosophers, and the people they influence, have no agreed methods of settling their disputes. Moreover, the parties to a religious or philosophic dispute rarely agree that neither is correct. Hence, when they are politically powerful, they always try to compel others to accept their views. Even in the United States today there is wide-spread intellectual censorship and coercion, achieved largely through economic and social pressure rather than by law. Thus most voters, soldiers, and government employees are still required to take a religious oath, including the phrase, "So help me God." and atheists are often not allowed to testify in court.

Since scientists have reliable methods of reaching agreement, they can be courteous and fair in their controversies.

Like other men, scientists often behave too emotionally when arguing, but, unlike priests and philosophers, they do not have to use epithets, sophistry, evasion, and coercion to win arguments. They alone have other means of reaching agreement. It is paradoxical but true that the priests who preach love and charity are much less likely than scientists to love or be charitable to those who disagree with them. When they were able, they burned them at the stake Today many of them preach a holy war against the atheist government of Russia. By contrast, modern scientists are trying to discover scientifically why men become communists and how well communism is working in Russia. They hate neither communists nor criminals because they believe that the worst that can be said of them is that they have been produced by a bad education and/or a bad social environment.

That scientists can succeed, where priests have failed, in persuading men who differ culturally to agree is well illustrated by the fact that during the last 150 years Asiatics have rapidly adopted Western science while at the same time they have almost completely rejected the religious and philosophic ideas so persistently forced upon them by Western missionaries. Scientific missionaries have been much less numerous than religious missionaries, but the former have been vastly more successful because the truths of science are verifiable, meaningful, and useful. For this reason, the acceptance of Western science by Asiatics is certain to continue to grow rapidly, while the small successes of religious missionaries are not likely to be repeated and may be largely wiped out.

E. Remnants of Pre-scientific Ideas in Science

Modern or sophisticated science is barely 400 years old. For the first 300 of these 400 years, scientific research was done only in Europe, was virtually limited to the so-called "natural sciences," was carried on by less than 1% of educated men, themselves a very small minority, and was grossly neglected in all European universities. Those few pioneers who engaged in it rarely had any formal training in research and had all been indoctrinated from early childhood with the unscientific and antiscientific dogmas of religion and philosophy. Moreover, they were usually afraid to criticize religion. There has been great improvement in the last century, but most of these obstacles to scientific thinking are still important, especially the last two. Consequently, many remnants of pre-scientific ways of thinking are still to be found in recent scientific publications. In the following pages we shall note and briefly criticize a few of these remnants of religion and philosophy.

1. *The Terms* Law *and* Nature

Perhaps the best illustration of the effects of religion and philosophy upon modern science is the continued use of the term *law* to denote a scientific truth. Modern science began as natural philosophy, and most natural philosophers accepted without question the traditional idea that events are controlled by divine or metaphysical laws. Theologians, idealistic philosophers, Catholic scientists, and many Protestant scientists still believe this. More enlightened scientists are of course well aware that scientific theories describe rather than control events, but they continue to use the term *law*, which clearly implies the opposite. They do so to avoid or reduce the criticism of science by religious people, who control nearly all universities. For the same reason, some scientists use the word *god* to denote the impersonal universe they study. Unfortunately such practices deceive not only religious critics of science but also many relatively open-minded students. It is always confusing to redefine old terms in a new way, particularly to mean the opposite of the old sense. Hence, the use of the term *scientific law* should be abandoned by consistent scientists as soon as it is safe to do so.

The false but very old and popular idea that scientific theories ("laws") determine, rather than describe, the course of events can be stated or implied in many ways. For instance, the philosopher, A. N. Whitehead, speaks of "general principles which *reign* throughout the natural order."

The mistaken belief that scientific theories govern events has led many conservatives to argue that government officials cannot or should not violate economic laws. Since the economic laws to which they refer are mere descriptive generalizations, they cannot be violated; they can only be corrected or disproven. Indeed every so-called violation of them proves that they are incorrect. This is the last thing that conservatives are willing to admit, for their economic laws are often merely statements of what they want to believe.

It is true, of course, that applied sciences contain many prescriptive rules which one can apparently obey or disobey. However, they merely describe how desired results can be achieved. Such rules can be used, but they cannot be obeyed. One obeys persons and laws (commands), not useful practical theories.

Another remnant of pre-scientific thought in the literature of modern science is the common use of the term *nature* and its derivatives. Philosophers have long used these terms to ask meaningless questions about the "nature" of truth, virtue, reality, etc. But they are not the only ones to use these terms meaninglessly. School teachers often tell students that dogs bark because it is natural for them to bark or that work makes us tired because this is natural. And many scientists have praised or admired the ways of nature, Nature, or Mother Nature. Even the most objective scientists often say that they are studying nature or natural phenomena.

To speak of the *world of nature* or the *natural order* implies that there is one or more other worlds or orders. To call some events *natural* suggests that there are *supernatural* events. To call all events *natural* makes the term meaningless since the statement that they are all natural is unverifiable. A noun or an adjective should be used only to distinguish between one thing and another.

It is true, of course, that *nature* and *natural* can be defined meaningfully. Thus we can define *nature* as the sum of all non-human things, and we can call things and events natural when they are non-human. But such use is ambiguous, because *natural* is also the opposite of *artificial, unnatural,* and *supernatural,* and it is never necessary since there are unambiguous synonyms. To be meaningful and unambiguous, scientists should therefore abandon the use of the term *nature* and all its derivatives, except when criticizing unscientific ideas.

Phrases like *law of nature, natural law,* the *rule of nature,* etc., combine the errors noted in our discussion of the term *nature* with those noted in our criticism of the term *scientific law.* Yet many professors of juisprudence and social science teach that the laws of the state should be based upon natural law. The American federal constitution and nearly all state constitutions are based upon this meaningless theory of natural law, and its corollary, the theory of natural rights.

2. *The Terms* Force *and* Energy

A third illustration of the harmful effects of religious and scientific reasoning upon modern science is the continued use by scientists of the terms *force* and *energy* and their synonyms and derivatives.

When men began to study inanimate objects, they

thought that these objects resembled animals. They believed that the movements of inanimate objects were due to vital forces. This idea goes back to primitive religious animism. It explains why men introduced the term *force* into physics. Later, physicists substituted the idea of *natural force* for that of *vital force,* which amounted to an advance from animism to metaphysics. Eventually, scientists defined *natural force* as the product of mass times acceleration (*ma*). This definition implies that *force* is not the name of an invisible entity which makes objects move, but a great many scientists and laymen still use the term *force* and thus suggest such an entity.

Physicists define *energy* verbally as the capacity to do work. To measure it, they multiply force (itself a mere product of multiplication) by the distance *(s)* over which the force is exercized, i.e., by a measure of how far an object continues to accelerate. Thus E — *f* x *s or ma* x *s.*

These verbal definitions of *force* and *energy* reveal that these nouns are the names of quantities obtained by multiplying two or three measurements of the same thing, not the names of entities. *Force* and *energy* have no objective nonmathematical referents. There is nothing observable to which they refer.

Unfortunately, the use of the nouns *force* and *energy* inevitably suggests that they have referents. Thus many men, including some eminent physicists, have asserted that the world consists partly or wholly of force or energy, as if these were distinct substances rather than mere products of multiplication. They ought to say that the world consists of massive moving things, not force or energy.

The nouns *mass* and *acceleration* are also objectionable because they have no nonmathematical, nonverbal referents. Physicists do not observe and measure entities denoted by *mass* and *acceleration.* Instead, they measure how massive an observed object is and how fast it accelerates.

If physicists use such nouns only in order to state their theories more briefly and/or simply, they can achieve the same result by using algebraic symbols—f for force, m for mass, etc., This is not misleading, for an algebraic symbol does not suggest a corresponding entity. Many men have said that the world consists of mass and energy, but few, if any, are likely to say that it consists of m and E.

There are many other physical terms—*work, inertia, specific gravity, potential energy,* etc.—which merely name mathematical products obtained by measuring the referents of meaningful nouns and then multiplying, dividing, adding or substracting the resulting measurements. The statements containing such terms are always senseless and misleading, but they can easily be replaced by statements containing only the names of the referents measured, their measurements, and appropriate algebraic symbols.

Since the terms *force* and *energy* have no referent or image, it is meaningless to speak of the conservation of energy. Only things can be conserved. We know that certain kinds and amounts of mechanical action, like friction, cause certain kinds and amounts of chemical or electrical changes. But this does not prove the existence of a metaphysical substance which remains unchanged in form and amount. And those scientists who realize this and still use the phrase, *conservation of energy,* to describe what does occur are guilty of using misleading language.

This criticism is equally valid when applied to the most recent versions of conservation theory. It is as misleading to speak of the *conservation of mass-energy* as to speak of the *conservation of energy.*

Our criticism of the terms *force* and *energy* also applies to all phrases including these terms, such as *the force of gravitation, magnetic force,* and *electrical energy.* And it cannot be evaded or answered by using *gravitation, magnetism,* or *electricity* in place of these phrases. *Gravitation, magnetism,* and *electricity* are nouns, and nouns should be used only to denote observable objects or events. We can observe gravitational, magnetic, electrical, and red things, but not gravitation, magnetism, electricity, or redness. We should use adjectives, not nouns, to describe how objects or events are qualified. It is proper to speak of gravitational movements and red objects, but not of gravitation and redness. Use of the noun *gravitation* implies an observable referent and suggests such erroneous conclusions as the belief that gravitation causes objects to fall to the earth. This common belief is as absurd as the belief that redness makes objects red or that the dormitive power of opium puts men to sleep.

It is possible to reply that modern physicists who use the term *gravitation* are well aware that there is no such thing as gravitation, that when they say gravitation causes some event they do not mean what they say, and that therefore their thinking is not metaphysical. This is often true, but scientists ought to say what they think as clearly as possible. Failure to do this has resulted in much confusion and error.

Bertrand Russell has written that, "Electricity is not a thing like St. Paul's Cathedral; it is a way in which things behave." We accept the first statement but not the second. A noun should not be used to denote the way things behave. If a thing behaves electrically or moves rapidly, we should speak of electrical behavior or rapid movement, not of electricity or rapidness.

In his book, *The Growth of Scientific Ideas* (1954), Wm. P. D. Wightman asserts that Einstein rendered "the concept of *force* redundant" by developing his general theory of relativity. But the concept of impersonal physical force is meaningless as well as redundant. And this more important conclusion is the result of semantic analysis, and could have been arrived at independantly of Einstein. In fact, it probably was arrived at before Einstein. The followers of Descartes, for instance, criticized Newton's theory of gravitation over 200 years ago because it was usually stated in terms of *force* or *attraction*, which they regarded as "occult" rather than scientific terms.

3. *The Terms* Attract *and* Repel

Scientists often claim that inanimate objects like stars or electrons attract or repel each other. This is a remnant of animism or metaphysics because such behavior cannot be observed. Men can feel attracted or repulsed, and it is conceivable that other living beings have such feelings, but there is no reason to think that inanimate objects have such feelings. The belief that inanimate objects have human emotions and sensations is animism. And the belief that they attract or repel is metaphysics. These beliefs are unverifiable and therefore nonsensical. Scientists should report or predict only what can be observed or verified, namely that stars or electrons move together or apart or otherwise.

4. *The Terms* Matter *and* Reality

The term *matter* is far more suitable for scientific use than the term *force*. Its introduction into physics was not due to animism or metaphysics. However, it has been given a special metaphysical (i.e. nonsensical) definition by certain philosophers. It has been used by philosophic materialists as the name for the ultimate reality behind appearance, i.e., for the noumena behind phenomena. Hence, when scientists use the term, they should explain that they are not using it in this philosophic sense (non-sense) but are using it instead to describe some observable thing or things, such as atoms, elements, molecules, etc. Only when it has an greed referent is the noun *matter* meaningful.

Once when answering questions at a forum on religion, the physicist, Robt. A. Millikan, was asked what he meant by the word *spirit*, which he had used repeatedly. He replied that if his questioner would define *matter* he would define *spirit*. His questioner was too shy or too uninformed to define *matter*, and Millikan thus evaded his question. If Millikan could not define matter, the numerous sentences in which he has used that term are meaningless. If he could define it, and asked for a definition from his interrogator only to disclose his ignorance or to evade answering a legitimate question, he was obscuring rather than disclosing the truth.

In commenting upon this incident later *(Evolution in Science and Religion*, p. 18), Millikan asserted that "it is today quite as difficult to find a satisfactory definition of 'matter' as of 'spirit.'" One wonders then why scientists use the term *matter* and not the term *spirit*. If these terms are equally meaningless, they should both be abandoned.

Like the term *matter*, the term *reality* is defined one way by philosophers and another way by scientists. To a philosopher, *reality* denotes the *unobservable* ground behind appearances. To a scientist, *reality* denotes what he verifiably observes. The fact that the term *reality* has been defined in these radically different ways is often ignored. For instance, Prof. H. Margenau has argued that science is paradoxical because it "will tell us what things are real but will refuse to say what is reality" *(The Nature of Physical Reality*, 1950). This seems to be a paradox only because the author first uses *real* to mean publicly observable and then uses *reality* to denote unobservable things. To avoid confusion, scientists should probably cease using terms like *reality* and *matter* which are key words in so many meaningless philosophic arguments.

5. *The Terms* Space *and* Time

It is said that Einstein has shown that the terms *absolute space* and *absolute time* are meaningless. In making this point, most writers stress the adjective *absolute* and continue to use *time* and *space* as if they were meaningful. But what do these nouns refer to? No operations can be conceived which will measure, reveal, or point to any thing or event which is a referent for these nouns. Hence, the bare nouns *time* and *space* are as nonsensical as the phrases *absolute time* and *absolute space.* Objects are related spatially and temporally, but there is no such thing as time or space. To use *time, space,* or *space-time continuum* as a noun is as illogical as to use *lateness* or *redness* as a noun.

Some scientists have defined *time* as what clocks measure. But clocks do not measure an unobservable homogeneous substance called time; they measure all events. Yardsticks do not measure a metaphysical or physical entity called space; they measure land or man-made objects. *Time* and *space* are meaningless nouns. They cannot be observed and they cannot be defined as similar to things which have been observed.

For these reasons, one should never say that events occur in time or space. Moreover, one should not say that events are spatial or temporal. No non-spatial or non-temporal events have ever been observed. Adjectives which apply to everything are as meaningless as those which apply to nothing. On the other hand, it is meaningful to ask how particular objects and events are related spatially or temporally because there are many different verifiable answers to such questions.

In daily speech, the words *space* and *time* often seem meaningful because they are used improperly as synonyms for meaningful terms. For instance, in the sentence, "My house occupies 600 square feet of space," the word space is used as a synonym for *level ground* or *land.* Again in the sentence, "He will come in time," the phrase *"in time"* is a synonym for *eventually.* Thus, when the words *space* and *time* seem meaningful, they can usually be replaced by other more suitable words. However, such a substitution of words is not possible in profound philosophic problems as to the nature of space, time or the space-time continuum. And most supposedly scientific problems about space, time, and the space-time continuum are in fact philosophic problems. In these pseudo-problems it is impossible to replace the words *time* and *space* with meaningful synonyms, because no verifiable answer to these problems can be conceived.

If *space* and *time* do not denote events or objects, it is pointless to investigate whether space is three or four-dimensional, straight or curved, finite or infinite. Moreover, the term *four-dimensional* is meaningless when applied to any object, for there is no way to determine by observation whether any given object is or is not four-dimensional. If the adjective *four-dimensional* applies by definition to all objects, it is meaningless because it does not distinguish between objects. And the fact that such terms may have an arbitrary verbal definition in mathematics is irrelevant. Much the same analysis applies to the adjectives *finite* and *infinite* (see pp. 102-04 above).

The above analysis of words like *force, attraction,* and *time* can be applied to many other terms used by chemists and physicists. For instance, the nouns *mass, weight, heat, cold, affinity, light, inertia, chance, probability, electric charge,* and *magnetism* are all senseless. Most of them can be used as, or transformed into, meaningful adjectives, adverbs, or verbs, but their use as basic nouns has often confused scientists. Thus the use of the word *heat* as a noun was party responsible for a prolonged effort to discover a substance which makes things hot when it flows into them.

Some positivists have said that although scientific nouns like *force* and *mass* have no referents, they can be used to state principles from which verifiable conclusions, which contain nouns having referents, can be deduced. We do not think this is a sufficient reason for using referentless nouns. We are convinced that all useful theories containing such nouns can be restated more clearly without using them. For instance, instead of saying that the force of impact of a moving billiard ball upon a non-moving one depends upon the mass and force of the first, we may say that the resulting movement of the struck billiard ball depends upon how much the other ball weighs, how fast it is moving when it strikes, and how squarely it hits the struck ball.

Our discussion of the terminology of modern physics and chemistry has necessarily been superficial and incomplete. Nevertheless it suggests that the application of our semantic rules to this terminology would markedly change and clarify the basic theories of these sciences. We believe this would make it much easier not only to learn and teach these sciences but, most important, would help the creation of new theories.

6. *The Terms* Id, Ego *and* Superego

We shall now turn briefly from physics to psychology. During the last fifty years, Freudian theories have been more widely discussed than any other psychological theories. Some of Freud's theories illustrate perfectly the nonsense and confusion that results from using referentless nouns. For instance, he taught that human conduct is strongly influenced by three often conflicting entities, the *id,* the *ego,* and the *superego.* The *id* demands immediate instinctive or sensual gratification. The *ego* suggests the most practical means, and sometimes advises delay in such gratification. The *superego* condemns and represses immoral desires. Freud also speaks of *the unconscious,* into which the superego represses these desires.

But no person can be divided into three independent actors. A man's conduct is determined by a single brain or nervous system. Human ends may perhaps be usefully divided into three partly conflicting classes—immediate want satisfaction, maximum long-run want satisfaction, and public approval. Or human conduct may perhaps be usefully divided into three such classes—instinctive, rational, and conscientious. Freud's discussion of the *id, ego,* and *superego* is literally senseless, because these terms have no referents or images, but his discussion suggests the above two classifications, among others.

For similar reasons, terms like *the unconscious, repression, compulsion,* and *obsession* are senseless. There are unconscious mental and nervous processes, but there is no mental storehouse which may usefully be called the unconscious. Conduct may be compulsive or obsessive, but there are no entities, denoted by *compulsion* and *obsession,* which cause or result from such conduct.

Libido is another senseless Freudian term. It seems to refer to the cause of libidinous behavior, but there is no single cause of such behavior. It would be equally unreasonable to coin a term like *kinda* and use it to denote a single cause of all kind behavior.

Freud's language may be graphic, vivid, startling, or suggestive, but it is quite unscientific. The key terms have no sensible referents or images and therefore no method of verifying statements containing them can be conceived.

For instance, there is no conceivable way of verifying the claim that the superego has repressed an incestuous desire and made it unconscious. Indeed, the term *unconscious desire* is self-contradictory because a desire must be conscious to be a desire.

Since Freud's theories are graphic and symbolic rather than literal and precise, they suggest several, sometimes many, possible verifiable hypotheses. Future psychologists who wish to utilize his theories will have to restate them as literal, sensible hypotheses and then try to verify them. To do this, they will have to talk about observable or reportable conduct, feeling, thinking, etc., rather than about entities like the id, ego, superego, and unconscious.

For instance, one might restate the basic Freudian doctrine as the theory that much if not most human behavior is instinctive (emotional) or conscientious rather than rational, and that men are happier and fare better when they behave rationally (expediently). The task of the psychoanalyst then becomes to help men become more rational and less impulsive and conscientious. When thus restated in literal, sensible terms, Freudian doctrine will appear much less original and striking, but, if verified, will be much more useful.

7. *Other Meaningless Terms Used by Scientists*

We would like to devote as much space to every science as we have given to physics. Since this is not practical, we shall merely enumerate some of the most commonly used meaningless words peculiar to the other major sciences. Workers in these other fields, of course, use many of the terms we have already criticized—*law, reality, time,* etc.—but we shall not repeat them for each science.

The nouns most often used meaninglessly by biologists, include *life, vitality, soul, vital force, entelechy, structure, form, heredity, vital power, evolutionary purpose, instinct, drive,* and *trait.* Partly because of the use of such nouns, biologists have wasted a great deal of money trying to answer meaningless questions concerning the nature of life, death, and vitality, the purpose of evolution, the location of the soul or vital force, etc.

Nouns most often used meaninglessly by psychologists include *soul, self, personality, spirit, mind, group mind, morale, mob psychology, faculty, role, consciousness, ego, super-ego, id, psychosis, neurosis, the unconscious, insanity, complex, will, will power, drive, want, desire, emotion, conscience, motive, memory, purpose, intelligence, habit,* and *attitude.* Of course, some of these nouns can also be used meaningfully.

Many psychologists are still working on the senseless problem of whether the mind is spiritual or physical, which can be stated in various ways, all equally senseless. Some of them take seriously meaningless problems as to the nature of conscience, the origin of consciousness, how acts of free will are related to bodily movements, how instinct differs from reason, etc.

Many psychologists used to explain why superior men are able to do certain things by asserting that certain faculties called *attention, memory, imagination, reasoning, will, industry, energy,* etc., exist and that when they are combined properly in a given person he is able to do certain notable things. For example, literary "ability" was supposed to be due to possessing a large amount of the faculties called *intellect* and *imagination.* This explanation is philosophic rather than scientific, and is a typical result of using nouns to describe so-called qualities.

Among the usually meaningless nouns in political science are *liberty, freedom, rule of law, power, state, sovereignty, authority, divine right, natural law, natural right, duty, will of the people, justice* and *public welfare.* The most popular meaningless questions are those concerning the nature of the state, the source of sovereignty, the criteria of natural rights, and the nature of justice. These points are elaborated in T. D. Weldon's *Vocabulary of Politics.*

In political economy we find such usually meaningless nouns as *economic value, utility, disutility, average cost, long-run supply, long-run price, productivity, perfect competition, monopoly, demand, exploitation, supply, elasticity, credit, velocity,* and *self-interest.* The most popular meaningless questions are those concerning the nature of value, the determination of average cost, the violation of natural economic laws, and the ethical virtues of competition.

In sociology we meet usually meaningless nouns or noun phrases like *society, social structure, social status, culture, in-*

stitution, security, custom, group emotion, social norms, social distance, social bond, social value, social organism, social purpose, social force, social consciousness, and *social duty.* Sociologists have often discussed such meaningless questions as the meaning of the social process, the nature of a social organism, and how far it is ethically right to reduce the legal rights of the individual in order to benefit society.

In recent decades there has been a great deal of argument among social scientists as to whether the individual is prior to society or vice versa. This whole controversy is either meaningless or trivial. John Dewey explains that, "To talk about the priority of 'society' to the individual is . . . nonsensical metaphysics. But to say that some pre-existent association of human beings is prior to every individual is to mention a commonplace." We would argue for these same conclusions by noting that the nouns *society* and *the individual* have no referent. And when one substitutes meaningful terms for them, in order to make clear what one thinks the author may have intended to say, the result is a trivial truism. The analysis of apparently profound social problems and theories often yields such results.

One very important qualification to our criticism of terms used by scientists should be added. Most of the nouns we have criticised have been created by transforming meaningful verbs, adverbs, or adjectives into nouns. In this they differ completely from typical basic religious and philosophic terms—*revelation, spirit, soul, reality, phenomena, essence, reason,* etc.—which were not created in this way.

When a scientist uses a senseless noun derived from a sensible verb, adverb, or adjective, it is usually possible to guess what he intends or ought to say and restate his sentence meaningfully by using the verb, adverb, or adjective from which his senseless noun is derived (see p. 24 above). Thus the senseless statement, "There is electricity in my room" can be transformed into the sensible statement, "There are electrically charged objects in my room." However, this cannot be done with statements containing words like *hell, angel, demon, spirit, force,* and *gravitation.*

Moreover, the sentence, "There are electrically charged objects in my room," is neither the equivalent nor a translation of the statement, "There is electricity in my room." There are no agreed rules of translation that permit us to translate one sentence into the other. Hence, the fact that one sentence is verifiable does not prove that the other is meaningful.

It may be replied that, whether or not there are agreed rules for translating such unverifiable statements into verifiable ones, scientists have agreed to consider them translatable into or equivalent to specific verifiable statements. This may be true. However, this answer implies that scientists could justify many apparently absurd theories merely by agreeing that they are the equivalent of sensible, verifiable theories. We believe this would be a highly confusing and very undesirable practice.

In our criticism of referentless scientific nouns, like *force* and *utility,* we have gone far beyond the orthodox logical positivist position. Most contemporary positivists are willing to let scientists use any accepted scientific term. All that they insist upon is that scientists begin with observation and end up with conclusions for which some method of verification can be conceived. This is certainly the fundamental thesis of positivism, but we believe that the application of the stricter semantic rules we have supported would also help greatly to end philosophic reasoning by scientists.

It should perhaps be noted that while we have criticised many widely used scientific terms on the ground that they are referentless, we do not believe that all referentless nouns are meaningless. In our Introduction, we explained that composite nouns are meaningful even though they are referentless. They cannot be used in true affirmative scientific statements but they can be used in hypotheses and in statements describing the negative results of tests of hypotheses containing them. For instance, if the word *ether,* is meaningfully defined, and we think some definitions of it are meaningful, it is possible to conceive of tests which would verify certain statements about ether or its effects. Thus while we have ruled out nouns like *force* and *time* as meaningless, we do not rule out *ether* or similar hypothetical nouns.

Anatol Rapoport has claimed that the chief if not the sole distinction between his operational philosophy and logical positivism is that the later rules out all referentless nouns like *ether*. We believe this is a false distinction.

F. Examples of Unscientific Reasoning

We have been illustrating the thesis that religion and philosophy have harmed science, especially physics, by showing that many common scientific terms are meaningless and/or have philosophic implications. We shall now illustrate the same basic thesis by offering examples of religious and philosophic thinking on supposedly scientific problems by a few famous scientists. We begin with Alfred Einstein because he is generally considered the greatest modern scientist, not because he is unusually guilty of unscientific reasoning. Indeed, his greatest achievement, the general theory of relativity is due to his recognition of the philosophic elements in previous supposedly scientific reasoning about time and space. Unfortunately, however, Einstein often appears unable to detect philosophic reasoning and distinguish it from scientific thinking in physics.

In *The Evolution of Physics* (1938), for instance, Einstein and Infeld claim that the progress of science has refuted the philosophic theory that the world is mechanical (pp. 57-9). But, if a theory can be proven or disproven by scientific research, it is a scientific theory, not a philosophic theory. In fact, it is quite meaningless to say that the world is mechanical or non-mechanical, for adjectives become senseless when applied to everything. Hence, scientists cannot prove or disprove that the universe is mechanical.

Einstein and Infeld believe in "the inner harmony of our world" (p. 313) but do not explain how this can be observed. The noun *harmony* is nonsensical because it has no agreed referent or image. The adjective *inner* suggests the meaningless philosophic distinction between outer appearance and inner reality. The adjective *harmonious* is also meaningless unless there are unharmonious things from which harmonious things can be distinguished. But if both unharmonious and harmonious things are observed, how can we discover which determines the "inner" world? Such questions are philosophic rather than scientific. Every scientist ought to be able to distinguish between the two and ought to denounce the former as nonsensical.

In *The Universe of Dr. Einstein* (1948), Lincoln Barnet asserts that Einstein has helped to solve the problem of whether scientists are in touch with "reality," presumably the reality behind appearance that philosophers talk about. This is a typical philosophic problem. It is impossible to conceive of any method of verifying any answer to it.

Bohr and Heisenberg claim that the fact that observation of an electron changes its behavior proves that the mysterious metaphysical boundary between the object and the subject has broken down. Thus they imply that a philosophic problem has been partly solved by scientific research.

Another example of this error is the argument that the progress of physics during the past 50 years has radically changed the scientific conception of matter and has therefore refuted the old philosophic theory of materialism. We have noted that the philosophic theory of materialism, like all philosophic theories, is meaningless. It follows that it cannot be supported or refuted by any new scientific research.

Robert Millikan, speaking of Galileo's brilliant pioneer work, claimed that, "Through it mankind began to know a God not of caprice and whim . . . but a God who works through law." Naturally he did not appeal to Heisenberg's principle of indeterminacy. However, he did assert that men have 'freedom of the will,' which implies that a vast range of phenomena is capricious.

The effect of childhood indoctrination with religion upon the conclusions of adult scientists is also illustrated in Eddington's popular book, *The Nature of the Physical World.* In order to undermine the theory of scientific determinism, and thus protect the religious theory of freedom of the will, he denied that the theory of gravitation applies to the behavior of the earth and concluded that "the earth goes anyhow it likes." He did not suggest any experiment to verify this remarkable hypothesis.

In this same book, Eddington argued that since we are as yet unable to explain scientifically the behavior of atoms and electrons, we may conclude that they are not subject to law at all but in fact have a sort of "free will" of their own. He also supported the inconsistent conclusion that when atoms are in a human body their action may be governed by a different "free will," i.e., that of the spirit in this body.

We have already noted that so-called scientific laws do not *govern* phenomena. The alternatives suggested by Eddington, namely that atoms have free will or are controlled by human will are both nonsensical because no possible method of testing them can be conceived.

Another physicist well known for his efforts to use science to support religion is James Jeans. In *The Mysterious Universe* he argued that, because geometry applies to the world, the world must have been constructed by a geometer. Bertrand Russell says, "Eddington deduces religion from the fact that atoms do not obey the laws of mathematics. Jeans deduces it from the fact that they do." We need only add that both conclusions are senseless because they are unverifiable.

The biologist Lloyd Morgan is famous for his doctrine of emergent evolution. "Emergent evolution," he says, "is from first to last a revelation and manifestation of that which I speak of as Divine Purpose." Unfortunately, he was unable to suggest any experiments which might test this hypothesis. Such neglect of verification is common among religious scientists, and it harms their scientific work as well as their treatment of personal, family, and social problems.

James B. Conant, chemist and ex-president of Harvard, has written a widely read book *On Understanding Science*. He treats science as but one of many varieties of truth. Apparently he accepts the claims of both theologians and philosophers that they can discover truth by non-scientific methods. On the second page of his preface he quotes approvingly a brief statement of Emerson's theory of compensation:

> . . . Evey excess causes a defect, every defect an excess . . . Every faculty which is a receiver of pleasure has an equal penalty put on its abuse . . . With every influx of light comes new danger. . . . There is a crack in everything God has made.

This is a perfect example of meaningless reasoning. There is no conceivable way of verifying the theory of compensation because it is nonsensical. To start a book on understanding science with an endorsement of a meaningless, unscientific theory is most confusing.

Since Conant wants to believe such philosophic theories, it is easy to explain his latter statement that "With any idolatry of science . . . I have little sympathy." What he means by idolatry of science is presumably positivism. The use of the prejudicial and inaccurate term *idolatry* is of course quite unscientific.

On the whole, Conant's book suggests that he is a Christian who uses scientific methods only in his laboratory rather than a scientist who applies such methods to all problems. Indeed, if he were a consistent scientist, he would probably never have been chosen as President of Harvard, for most of the trustees of Harvard are religious men.

In *The Nature of the Universe* (1950) the astronomer, Fred Hoyle, attacked "materialists" (positivists?) for claiming that such questions as "why is the universe here at all?" are meaningless. He argued that scientists have often solved problems long considered unsolvable, and concluded that instead of "throwing up the sponge" we should try to find out "Why the universe is as it is . . ." and "Why it is here at all."

Hoyle seems unaware that such questions have both a philosophic or religious interpretation and a scientific one. The positivist does not question the possibility of solving these problems interpreted as scientific problems. However, he is aware that these problems may be interpreted as non-scientific problems and that when so interpreted they are meaningless and unsolvable. Hoyle simply does not know what makes a question scientific, and why "materialists" object to non-scientific questions.

G. The Claim that Some Scientific Theories Cannot Be Verbally Explained to Laymen

Some modern physicists claim that their latest theories cannot be explained to educated laymen. Sometimes they assert that these theories can only be stated as abstruse mathematical propositions. At other times, they seem to believe that the words they use—*four dimensional space-time continuum, electric field, energy,* etc.—cannot be defined so that laymen will understand them. We believe that one reason it is difficult to define these terms is that they are often meaningless. It should be possible to explain any meaningful theory to laymen because such a theory is verifiable, and can be explained by describing how it can be verified.

Another reason why it is at times difficult to explain scientific theories is that they are stated in terms which mean one thing to scientists and something quite different to laymen. The term *law* is an example. Scientists ought to abandon such terms. For instance, they should substitute *theory* or *generalization* for law. It is proper to take common words and define them more strictly, but it is misleading to take words like *law* and *force* and define them quite differently. Moreover, as we have explained, this is often a remnant of pre-scientific thinking and has religious or metaphysical implications.

A third reason why some scientists cannot explain their theories to intelligent laymen is that they wish to include in their theories more than observation alone can verify. But conclusions should never go beyond what observation has supported. When they are thus limited, they are literal, prosaic, and relatively clear.

Some modern scientists believe that pure mathematics can replace verbal language in stating the higher or newer truths of physics and chemistry. Conant has asserted that mathematics is "the language of science." This is a serious error. Propositions which consist solely of mathematical symbols cannot describe the world. Such symbols have no referents. They cannot be defined by pointing to something. They can only be defined verbally in arbitrary axioms and definitions. The so-called "truths" of mathematics are not factual or scientific truths, but merely valid propositions and therefore, as we have noted (p. 89) should not be called truths.

When mathematics is applied to scientific problems, it yields statements in which some words are mathematical and some are not, like "Two oranges plus two oranges are four oranges." In such sentences, all the nouns should be non-mathematical and meaningful. Then the sentence may be meaningful. It is factually meaningless to say that "Two plus two are four" because "two" and "four" have no agreed referents or images, but it is meaningful to say that "Two oranges plus two oranges are four oranges" because this claim can be verified. Therefore, mathematics cannot replace language in stating scientific theories, regardless of how pure, abstract, or complex, these theories may be.

Modern physicists are far less skilled in the use of words than in the use of mathematical symbols. They need to learn how to express themselves clearly and effectively in words. They should study semantics, logical analysis, modern positivism, and related subjects.

". . . Men are always determined by *feelings,* and in such a manner that they always strive for that goal, among those considered, the idea of which is characterized, at the time of choice, by the least pain or the greatest pleasure . . ."

"What is the meaning of moral? . . . That conduct which society believes will best further its own welfare."

"If we put the two results together we see that the main problem, 'Why do men act morally?' will be solved as soon as we can show how the idea of the things which appear useful to society can also be pleasant for the individual agent himself."

Moritz Schlick, *Problems of Ethics* (1939), p. 160.

"Reason is wholly confined to adjusting the comparison between the different objects of desire and investigating the most successful mode of attaining these objects." Wm. Godwin (1798).

CHAPTER V. PERSONAL CONDUCT

A. *Introduction*

WE HAVE DESCRIBED in some detail how men reason religiously, philosophically, and scientifically. Men think or reason in order to act more wisely. Hence the most important fact about each method of reasoning is how it affects personal conduct. And the most significant intellectual problem is how we should reason when we are trying to act wisely or to persuade others to act wisely. We have dealt briefly and incidentally with these points in previous chapters. Now we shall devote an entire chapter to them. This amounts to a practical application of the general theories we have stated.

Theories of personal conduct seem to have gone through four historical stages of development: (1) naive science or primitive common sense, (2) religious morality, (3) philosophic ethics, and (4) sophisticated or modern applied science. Primitive men probably learned that it pays to be honest, loyal to one's group, friendly to other members of this group, courageous in repelling attacks upon it, etc., long before anyone suggested that they would be punished by spirits or gods for not being honest, loyal, friendly, courageous, etc. However, we know scarcely anything about this first stage in the development of theories of conduct and shall not discuss it in this chapter.

The theories of personal conduct contained in the oldest surviving literary works of the western world are primitive religious theories or rules like the ten commandments. Religious theories of conduct have been held by most peoples and thinkers for at least 5,000 years.

The first Western thinkers to abandon religious ethics and create new philosophic theories of conduct were the Greek sophists. Most Greek philosophers of course used philosophic reasoning primarily to reform or support orthodox religious ideas, including religious ethics, but a few radical thinkers abandoned religion completely and relied upon "reason" to create independent and original philosophies and ethical theories. The rise of Christianity virtually stopped such independent philosophizing for a thousand years, but it revived in the 16th century and became steadily more widespread and influential until about 1850.

Religious and philosophic theories of conduct are both called ethics. They have much in common, even though one is supposedly based upon revelation and the other upon reason. There are innumerable competing and conflicting theories of each type, and all of them are deductive, dogmatic, absolute, universal, undemonstrable, etc. For these reasons we shall criticize them together under a single heading, *ethics,* one of the two main divisions of this chapter.

Modern or sophisticated scientific theories of personal conduct are very new when compared with either religious or philosophic ethics. The general name for these new theories is applied science. Almost 90% of modern applied science has been created in the past century. Medicine is one of the oldest and most highly developed applied sciences, but a hundred years ago doctors knew less than 1% of what they know now about the cure of the sick.

Although modern applied science is largely new, it has already greatly changed personal conduct in advanced countries, especially among the more prosperous and better educated classes. Most Americans now go to the doctor rather than the priest for advice on diet, fasting, sexual relations, birth control, circumcision, and other health problems. Even the most religious usually go to the doctor first. Only after he has failed to cure them do they travel from shrine to shrine, or faith healer to faith healer, seeking a miraculous religious cure.

Nevertheless, most Americans still believe that ethical theories are needed to solve many of the most important and difficult problems of personal conduct. Indeed few men have ever heard this common opinion challenged.

The positivist theory of conduct is entirely different. The positivist believes that there are no moral problems, that all ethical or moral theories are meaningless, and that problems of personal conduct can be solved only by amoral scientific analysis. We shall now proceed to elaborate this criticism of ethics.

B. *Ethics*

1. *Definition of Ethics*

We use the words *ethics* and *morality* to describe all theories of personal conduct created and/or supported by means of religious or philosophic reasoning. Thus for us ethical problems are not those concerning certain classes of conduct, like sexual behavior, but those which have been treated and allegedly solved by religious and philosophic analysis. It is the method of reasoning, not the subject matter, which determines whether a theory or problem is ethical.

Religious ethics is nominally based upon revelation. The ten commandments, for instance are said to have been written on stone tablets by Jahweh himself. The Mormons believe that their bible was written on thin sheets of gold and buried in the ground for Joseph Smith to find. In numerous other cases, some god is claimed to have spoken directly to a man, who was then able to write or preach the divine truth revealed to him. In practice, of course, there is no way to tell whether a man who claims to be divinely inspired is telling the truth. Some are believed, some are crucified, and, in modern times, some are committed to insane asylums. Moreover, all revelations leave room for personal interpretation. For instance, the revelation that Christians should turn the other cheek has often been interpreted to mean that they should not turn the other cheek.

Philosophic ethics is based upon general principles allegedly disclosed by the light of reason. These basic ethical principles are *obviously* true to those who accept them, but not to those who reject them. Unfortunately, different men often claim that reason has revealed conflicting premises. Hence, there are numerous conflicting ethical opinions among philosophers, and no way of determining which is correct.

Both religious and philosophic ethics are entirely deductive. All applications to individual problems are deduced from revealed or rational principles. However, since there is an unlimited number of revealed or rational general principles to choose from, the individual can nearly always find one which will yield a desired conclusion. Thus pure deduction is consistent with wishful thinking.

John Dewey once defined ethics as "the science that deals with conduct, in so far as this is considered as right or wrong, good or bad." We have already explained why we do not consider ethics as science. Here we wish to criticize the use of the terms *good* and *bad* and their synonyms. These terms are highly ambiguous. For instance, a good picture is a beautiful one, a good tennis player is a skillful one, a good book is an interesting, informative, or uplifting one, etc. Dewey probably used *good* to mean *ethically good,* in which case his definition is a tautology.

It is sometimes claimed that ethics deals only with ends, that is with the problem of what moral ends men ought to seek. However, this is true only of certain philosophic ethical theories. Religious ethics has always consisted chiefly of rules which tell men what means they should use to achieve divine approval. One cannot be honest both because this is a moral end-in-itself and because this is a means of winning divine rewards. Indeed, religious teachers have frequently urged men to fight, kill, lie, or torture in order to aid true believers and/or to please some god. It is the philosophers, not the priests, who have often taught that to love, to be honest, or to be charitable is an end-in-itself, regardless of its effect upon any religious movement. However, most Christians have nominally accepted both the theory that the ten commandments are absolute and universal rules and the contradictory theory that these rules should be broken whenever this aids Christians to survive and preach their faith.

Ethical conduct must be clearly distinguished from expedient or prudent conduct. The former is thought to please some god or to make one virtuous, the latter benefits men observably and measureably. It makes men healthy, wealthy famous, and so forth. This distinction is ignored by some ethical thinkers, who argue that ethical conduct also benefits men observably. But the problem of how to achieve a desired observable result is always a problem in applied science. If moralists solve problems of conduct in the same way as applied scientists, there is no reason to call their work ethics instead of science and teach it in separate courses. And if they solve these problems in a different way and with different results, the important facts about ethics are those which distinguish it from applied science. *Unless ethical conduct differs from expedient conduct there is no need for ethics.*

Obedience to a rule of conduct may be expedient for the individual or for some group which includes him. When moralists distinguish between moral and expedient conduct they sometimes seem to identify moral conduct with conduct which is expedient for some group, usually the tribe or nation. The term *moral* seems meaningful and different from *expedient* when so used, but actually it means *expedient-to-*

a-group. This is a scientific term, for scientists can determine by observation what is expedient to a group.

While the criteria for determining ethical conduct are quite different from those for determining expedient conduct, ethical conduct may also be expedient. Many rules of expedient conduct which developed before ethical theories were created were taken over and endorsed by priests and philosophers.

It is also essential to distinguish between ethical and conventional conduct, i.e., between morals and mores. Practical men usually confuse the two. They consider unconventional behavior to be immoral and they approve of immoral behavior which is conventional. Moreover, social scientists occasionally identify morals with mores, especially when describing primitive tribes. In fact, however, ethics does not *describe,* it *prescribes,* behavior. The moralist says men should act in certain ways because this is ethical, not because it is conventional. However, the conduct they approve is often conventional, either because they have endorsed customary conduct or because they have determined it.

Ethical conduct differs as well from legal conduct. Many laws have been enacted to enforce generally accepted ethical rules, but in all countries some laws violate the ethical principles of some citizens. For instance, many Americans believe it is unethical to execute convicted felons, but the law requires this. Since ethical theories are steadily becoming more numerous and more varied, they conflict with the law more and more frequently. Moreover, conduct which is considered unethical is often quite legal.

2. *All Ethics is Meaningless*

It has long been recognized that ethical principles differ from country to country, from age to age, and from sect to sect. This has made many men doubtful of all ethical rules. To this old ground for ethical scepticism, logical positivists have added a very important new one. They assert that all ethical statements are literally meaningless or nonsensical because they are religious or philosophic. We have already stated in some detail the general theory as to why most religious and philosophic doctrines are senseless, so we shall not devote many more words to this point. However, a few sample analyses of common ethical ideas should help to show how vulnerable these ideas are to the new positivist criticism.

Every ethical principle is, or may be reformulated as, a sentence in which some kind of conduct is the subject and this subject is described in the predicate. The statement, "Stealing is immoral," is an example. We shall call an ethical doctrine formulated in this way a *simple ethical doctrine*. All such doctrines are meaningless because the predicate is nonsensical. Some of them also have a meaningless subject. We shall consider these two points separately, beginning with a criticism of ethical predicates.

a. Ethical Predicates

Ethical doctrines may be religious or philosophic. The religious moralist says that stealing is sinful or wicked, i.e., that it is disapproved by some god. The philosophic moralist says that it is unethical, immoral, etc., i.e., that it is contrary to reason. Both statements are meaningless because no method of verifying them can be conceived. There is no way to determine whether stealing is disapproved by some god and no way to determine whether it is contrary to reason. Of course, we can usually determine whether stealing is condemned by any given theologian or philosopher, but this is entirely different from determining whether it is in fact literally sinful or unethical.

We say the word *wicked* is senseless, because it is not factually meaningful. We do not thereby deny that its use implies something about the beliefs of the user. It is always vital to distinguish clearly between what a word or sentence means factually and what it implies about the speaker.

When we say that honest men earn more money than dishonest men, the hearer understands us because he can think of many ways of testing this claim. When we say that honest men are ethically good, he does not understand us because he can not imagine any way of checking this statement. The observable results of ethically good conduct are the same as the results of ethically bad conduct. If they differed, scientists could observe the different results, and the problem of distinguishing between ethically good and bad conduct would be a scientific problem.

In other words, if *ethically good* and *ethically bad* are defined so as to make statements including them verifiable, they become scientific terms and ethics becomes superfluous. If they are not so defined, they cannot be used in a verifiable and therefore meaningful sentence.

In practice, of course, we often say that a man is a good man if he obeys the laws, earns an honest living, and is kind to his family and friends. But this is a scientific, not an ethical, use of *good.* Law-observance, industry, and kind acts can be scientifically defined, observed, and measured. Moreover, scientists have already learned something about how to make men law-abiding, industrious, and considerate, and they will learn much more. This is applied science, not ethics.

The above analysis of *wicked* and *unethical* is of course equally applicable to all of their synonyms and antonyms—*right* and *wrong, moral* and *immoral, righteous* and *unrighteous, fair* and *unfair, equitable* and *inequitable, virtuous* and *wicked,* etc., when used as ethical terms. It follows that all nouns used to name morally good or bad conduct—*morality* and *immorality, virtue* and *wickedness, integrity, probity, honor, rectitude, uprightness, worth, sin, evil, vice, wrong,* etc.,—are also nonsensical when so used.

Most of these terms may be used differently and may

then be meaningful. For instance, *moral* or *morality* may be used meaningfully to denote meaningless rules of moral conduct. And terms like *just* and *equitable* can be used to mean *legal* or *according to law.*

It is possible, of course, to state any ethical theory without using the terms *sinful* or *unethical* or any of their synonyms or antonyms. For instance, a moralist can say that men *should* or *ought* to be honest, but all such formulations assume or imply that the recommended conduct is *ethically good.* In other words, all ethical doctrines stand or fall with the assumption that the term *ethically good* and its synonyms are meaningful.

Ethics includes many theories as to what conduct or law is just. The adjective *just* is used in various ways. We say a court verdict is just when it is verifiably true or when it is verifiably in accord with the law. We also say that such true or law-abiding decisions are unjust when we believe the law is unwise or immoral. We say that a father has treated his son justly if he has treated him as the law requires or as is customary. We also say that such law-abiding or customary treatment is unjust if we consider it unethical. We could cite many other cases in which *just* is used as a synonym for *ethical* as we have defined the latter. Therefore, our citicism of ethics applies to many theories of jurisprudence, political science, economics, etc. For instance, the theories that punishment for crime is just, or that slavery is unjust, or that producers should charge a just price, etc., may be ethical rather than scientific and, if ethical, subject to our criticism of ethics.

If all ethical predicates—*good* and *bad, right* and *wrong, righteous* and *wicked,* etc—are meaningless, why are they used so often? The answer is simple but extremely significant. First, when one says that certain conduct is bad, wrong, wicked, etc., he shows how he feels and thus satisfies himself emotionally, as he does when he says that he likes or loves a person. In both cases, he shows that he approves of something, but in the former case he does not say what he means; he only shows how he feels. Secondly, by calling an act morally good or bad, one indicates that he and others may reward or punish the actor.

b. Ethical Subjects

We have shown that the statement that certain conduct is or is not sinful or unethical is meaningless because the predicate is senseless. Many simple ethical theories also have meaningless subjects. We shall now discuss a few examples of such theories.

(1) *To Be Unselfish*

In some version or other, the rule that to be unselfish is morally good is one of the oldest and most widely accepted ethical doctrines. However, the term *unselfish is* always vague and often meaningless. It may be defined in one of many scientific ways, i.e., by using it to denote some class of observable actions. For instance, we may say a man who gives away 20% of his income each year or who adopts six or more children is unselfish. But in fact moralists who preach unselfishness have never been able to agree upon such a definition of the term.

In ordinary usage, *selfish* and *unselfish* describe why rather than how men act, but it is very hard to determine why men act as they do. We cannot observe what other men are thinking, nor can we depend upon their reports as to why they do something. Conscious motives, moreover, are often mere rationalizations. It is very easy to conceive and consciously accept motives which are socially approved rather than ones which are socially condemned. And how shall we classify a man who desires to benefit both himself and the community at the same time?

Although we usually cannot discover why men act, and

thus cannot classify their acts as selfish or unselfish, we can conceive of ways of determining scientifically the observable effect of human acts upon the actors and upon others. But this does not mean that it is possible to define selfish conduct as that which benefits the agent and unselfish conduct as that which benefits others. First, the effect is often different from what was intended, and it would violate common usage to say that a man acts unselfishly when he tries to benefit himself. Secondly, the great majority of acts benefit both the agent and the community. Thirdly, there are few acts which benefit the agent and harm the public. Most of those which men expect to do so, such as theft or discourtesy, do not usually do so. Prisons and skid rows are full of people who tried to benefit themselves at the expense of the community and failed. If we judge their mistaken conduct on the basis of results, we must call it unselfish. There are, of course, a few men who have succeeded in benefiting themselves by deliberately harming the community, but if we limited the meaning of selfish conduct to such acts, it would cover an extremely small class, and it would be very hard to determine which acts belonged in this class. Moreover, if people knew that all selfish acts were rewarded they would scarcely refrain from them.

In his famous *Fable of the Bees* (1705), Bernard de Mandeville was perhaps the first writer to argue that unselfish conduct usually injures, and selfish conduct usually benefits, society. His shocking conclusions were bitterly attacked by his contemporaries. However, Adam Smith used them as the basis for his *laissez faire* economic theory in 1776, and most modern economists believe that self-regarding economic conduct usually benefits both the individual and the community. Paradoxically, this economic view is also common among priests and philosophers who teach that to be selfish is always immoral, while the growing attack upon *laissez faire* doctrine has been led by materialists and atheists, like Marx and Engels.

While economists are unscientific if they assume that men are selfish, since there is no agreed way to distinguish between selfish and unselfish conduct, they are justified in teaching that men normally seek to increase their income, for this can be verified by observation.

There is a great deal more which might be said about the word *selfish.* But the above should suffice to make clear why this term and its synonyms and derivatives are vague and confusing, if not meaningless. Scientific thinkers should never use them except when warning others against such use or criticizing those who use them.

(2) *To Forgive*

Another old and still widely accepted ethical principle is that to forgive those who injure us is morally good. The new testament says that men should not only forgive their enemies repeatedly (seventy times seven) but should love them. Here again we have a very ambiguous key word. What does *to forgive* mean? It would be easy to show that numeous interpretations of it have been offered. Moreover, nearly all of those who accept the above doctrine have been quick to resist and repay attacks upon themselves, their family, and their country if able to do so safely.

The principles that we should forgive our enemies seems significant and plausible to many people because it can easily be misinterpreted to mean that it usually pays to forgive those who injure us. For instance, if a husband overlooks minor injurious acts by his wife, friends, and business associates, he may be happier and more prosperous. But it is very unwise to forgive criminals, dishonest business men, and bitter enemies if this means treating them like friends or overlooking their harmful acts.

Since conduct is determined by causes, men cannot react in the same way to harmful as to beneficial acts. They may briefly restrain their normal response to aggression, but this must inevitably make them feel nervous and frustrated. We do not believe men are capable of forgiving their enemies in the sense of treating them as friends.

Moreover, even if we could forgive our enemies in this sense, it would be very unwise to do so, for this would greatly increase crime and aggression. Our enemies include criminals at home and aggressors abroad. If we failed to resist and to penalize their assaults upon us, we should soon be paupers. No community which allowed criminals to run wild has ever survived.

There is another interpretation of the term *forgive* which makes preaching of forgiveness plausible. As we grow older, we remember less and less until we have largely forgotten the past, including many injuries and enemies. Moreover, men angered by insult or injury calm down faster than they forget. The ethical doctrine that men should forgive their enemies may be misinterpreted to suggest only that men should cool off and/or forget injuries as they normally do. In this case, of course, the doctrine is meaningful but superfluous.

Actually, it is probably useful to be able to remember injuries and benefits longer and more clearly than the average man. This enables one to discriminate longer and more accurately between his enemies and his friends and between large and small benefits and injuries. A perfectly wise man would remember perfectly all helpful and harmul acts and would treat those responsible for them in such a way as would induce men to be most helpful to him. He would also cooperate with his fellow citizens in social action to penalize anti-social acts and to eliminate their causes.

The theory that harmful acts should be forgiven in the sense of forgotten or ignored is as foolish as the theory that wages should have no relation to output. Both assume that conduct is not influenced by penalties and rewards.

It is a remarkable paradox that those who teach men to forgive usually believe in a future life in which all men will be punished or rewarded according to their deserts. They even urge forgiveness on the ground that their god will not forgive men if they are not forgiving.

(3) *Just Prices, Wages, and Interest Rates*

The fact that the subjects of simple ethical doctrines are often senseless may become more evident if we examine certain ethical doctrines which were once almost universally accepted by Christians but have now been generally abandoned except by Roman Catholic theologians. Let us consider the medieval ethical principle that every producer should charge a just price for his product or service. Reformulated as a simple ethical doctrine, it becomes, "to charge a just price is morally right."

Modern economic theory tells us how actual prices are determined and how ideal prices ought to be determined in order to maximize per capita real income. However, an ideal or optimum price is not an ethically just price. If it were, science and ethics would be identical, and ethics would be superfluous.

But if an economically ideal price is not an ethically just price, how can the latter be determined, and how can one prove that it is preferable to an economically ideal price? It has been claimed that a just price is one which assures a fair return to the producer, but this answer is a mere tautology. *Ethically just* and *ethically fair* are synonyms. It is as impossible to determine a fair return as to determine a just price. Terms like *just price* and *fair return* are senseless. Therefore it is impossible to prove that any price is just or any return is fair.

The same criticism applies to medieval ethical theories of a just wage and a just rate of interest. We can determine, or will in time learn to determine, economically ideal wages and interest rates, but it is impossible to determine ethically just wages and interest rates. Nevertheless, belief that the state can prescribe just prices, wages, and interest rates is still common.

(4) *Natural Rights*

The theory that men have certain inalienable natural rights—to be personally free, to speak and write freely, to worship or not worship freely, etc.—is an old philosophic doctrine. The theory that to ignore or violate such rights is unethical is a corollary of this doctrine. It is meaningless not only because the predicate is meaningless but also because the subject is nonsensical.

The term *natural right* includes an ambiguous adjective and a meaningless noun. The noun *right* cannot be directly or indirectly defined by pointing. As a result no statement about it can be checked by observation. The adjective *natural* is ambiguous because it is used as the opposite of unnatural, supernatural, preternatural, artificial, etc.

Those who believe in natural rights have never been able to agree on what should be called natural rights. Some moralists believe that women have a natural right to possess private property and others deny this. Some believe women have a natural right to divorce insane husbands and others deny this. We could quote such disagreements indefinitely. And moralists have no means of settling these disagreements precisely because the term *natural right* is meaningless. There is no conceivable way of demonstrating that anyone has a natural right to anything.

A natural right is not a legal right, a claim which is enforceable by law. Statements about legal rights can be verified, but those about natural rights cannot.

The authors of the American constitution believed that

all men have natural rights to life, liberty, and the pursuit of happiness. They also believed in and practiced human slavery. This did not violate their theory of natural rights because the theory is meaningless. If the philosophic theory that men have a natural right to be free means that human slavery is immoral, the able men who wrote the American constitution were either unaware of this or they deliberately chose to be hypocritical and immoral.

The recent controversy over freedom of speech in America shows how futile arguments over natural rights can be. The liberals have argued that every man has a natural right to express his opinion, and have pointed out that this right is affirmed in the Declaration of Independence and guaranteed by the Constitution. In their replies, the conservatives have failed to explain that the term *natural right* is nonsensical. Rather they have developed a philosophic answer to the senseless liberal argument. They admit that Americans have a natural right to express their ideas freely, but they claim that they have no right to keep their job after expressing unpopular ideas. In the words of *Life* Magazine, one of the most intelligent conservative periodicals, dissenters have a natural right to freedom of speech but they have "no inherent right to a job, least of all a government job" *(Life,* 12/22/52).

Instead of debating the existence of a natural right to freedom of speech or jobs, liberals and conservatives ought to debate whether it is socially expedient to control speakers and writers by depriving dissenters of their jobs. This would turn a meaningless ethical problem into a meaningful scientific problem.

John Dewey once defined ethics as the study of choice "as affected by the rights of others" in order "to judge it as right or wrong by this standard." This suggests again that he did not understand how sense differs from nonsense. It is as senseless to say that men have rights (other than legal rights) as to say that conduct is ethically right or wrong.

c. Do Ends Justify Means?

One of the most frequently discussed ethical problems is whether the end justifies the means. Most moralists assert that the end does not justify the means, and unpopular groups—Communists, Jesuits, Fascists, etc.,—are often accused of accepting the immoral theory that the end does justify any means necessary to achieve it.

In fact, this is a meaningless problem. As used here, *justify* means *to justify ethically,* i.e., unscientifically, and is therefore meaningless.

It is possible, of course, to ask meaningfully whether a certain means aids the achievement of a particular result, but this is a scientific, not an ethical, question. It can be settled by experiment or observation. A man who says that cruel persecution of a given political or racial group will achieve a specific result, such as the elimination of that group, is not a moralist because he has not said the end or the means is moral. He is stating a scientific hypothesis or truth. We know today that the Catholic Inquisition was successful in almost completely eliminating Protestants in certain areas. Whether this end justified the bloody means, however, is a senseless question to which no meaningful answer can be given. Catholics naturally tend to condone or approve, and Protestants to disapprove of these means. When they assert or deny that the end justified these means, they merely show that they personally like or dislike the results.

Every new law, like every economic act, benefits some persons and injures others. Whether it is beneficial or harmful depends upon whether the good results offset the bad. *All social and personal decisions which deserve careful consideration require a balancing of painful against pleasant results.* The question of whether an end justifies a particular means requires the same kind of balancing. If the painful or harmful results of using certain means outweigh the pleasant results of their use, they should not be used, and *vice versa.*

The sound argument against the Inquisition, or any other painful means, is not that the means were immoral, but that they caused some men to suffer so much that those who benefited could not have compensated them and still come off as net beneficiaries. In economics, this is called the principle of compensation. Actually, the Inquisition injured millions of men, many very seriously, and benefited relatively few. Hence, it was harmful, but not immoral or unjust.

Those who believe that the end does not justify the means are on the whole just as willing to use any means to achieve desired ends as those who teach the opposite. For instance, they burnt heretics by the millions to achieve a "good" end, the spread of their religion. They practised human slavery in the United States until 1864 in order to earn more money. They still execute criminals in order to deter others from crime. They deny government jobs to American citizens without a trial or hearing in order to protect American secrets. This list could be expanded indefinitely.

d. Might vs. Right

Moralists often claim that "right makes might." This claim is meaningless, but it suggests the claim that "conduct deemed morally right makes men and nations militarily strong." This doctrine has encouraged many men to do what they think is moral rather than what they think is expedient, but it is not an ethical doctrine because it is verifiable. It is possible to determine roughly what conduct men think is moral and then measure the effect of such conduct upon military power. However, it is not necessary to do this in order to prove that the doctrine is false. It is well known that moral doctrines vary widely from time to time and people to people, and often contradict each other. Thus, if behavior deemed morally right made a nation mighty, we would get the same results from different causes, which is impossible.

Some iconoclasts assert that "might makes right." This is meaningless because *might* and *right* are nouns which have no referents or images, but it suggests at least two meaningful statements, (1) that mighty men and nations usually prevail over weak men and nations who think their conduct is moral, and (2) when mighty classes or nations win a civil or international war, they often force the defeated to profess the moral doctrines favored by the winner. We think both statements are true.

It is science, not ethics, which makes a nation mighty, other factors being the same. Russia is a serious military threat to the United States because she has spent tremendous sums on scientific education and research, not because she has spent large sums on moral education and research. Every effort to turn a people from scientific thinking and research to ethical analysis and education makes it militarily weaker.

3. *Some Ethical Subjects are Too General*

We have explained why the subjects of some simple ethical doctrines are meaningless. There are of course many ethical subjects which are meaningful, or can be made meaningful, like *stealing, lying, murder,* etc. However, these meaningful ethical subjects are nearly all seriously defective because they are too general. We can illustrate this best by using one of them with a meaningful predicate. Let us consider the statement, "Stealing is inexpedient." This claim is obviously too general because stealing is sometimes expedient. It is impossible to prove that the statement, "Stealing is unethical," is too general because the predicate is meaningless, but with any meaningful predicate the subject becomes too general

As another illustration, let us consider the rule that "Killing men is unethical." Men kill in self-defense, in war, in duels, in crime, in suicide, in abortions, in accidents, when drunk, when insane, etc. The practical problem is always whether killing is proper under certain specific circumstances. Clearly it is often expedient. If the adjective *moral* were meaningful, killing would sometimes be moral. The same analysis can be applied to many other ethical subjects—adultery, lying, disobedience to parents, law-breaking, etc.

It may seem that this criticism can be answered by inserting appropriate adjectives, adverbs, or other modifiers in the statement criticized as too general. Thus we might say "most stealing is inexpedient" or "stealing is usually inexpedient." This is possible in a scientific but not in an ethical statement. Nor is it customary. The ten commandments would surely sound odd if they were all qualified in this way. "Thou shalt not usually commit adultery" not only sounds odd but it implies that adultery is not intrinsically wicked or immoral. Moral rules must be general. Since they are not based upon observation, they cannot be qualified so that they accord with observable results. As the conduct prescribed is an end-in-itself, it is always moral.

The philosopher Kant declared that, if we are asked by a murderer for the hiding place of our best friend, we should tell the truth, knowing that this would probably result in his death, because truth-telling is a moral virtue. When men stop to consider the results of truth-telling, they become prudent rather than ethical.

If democratic government is morally good, every nation should be democratic. Many Americans actually believe that Russia, China, and Abyssinia ought to have a democratic government now because they think it is immoral to be undemocratic. By contrast, social scientists are well aware that democratic government is the latest political development in a long evolution and that only a few politically advanced peoples are ready for it.

4. *How Ethical Rules Influence Conduct*

Ethical rules are literally meaningless because no method of verifying them can be conceived. Therefore, no one can be influenced in his conduct by what ethical statements literally assert. However, ethical rules often influence conduct because: (1) they suggest scientific statements which resemble them and which are meaningful, and because (2) those who state them often make clear that they themselves, employers, neighbors, and/or the police will try to enforce the recommended moral rules.

The doctrine that lying is unethical is usually stated more briefly as the claim that lying is wrong or bad. This suggests to many men the idea that lying is bad for business, a verifiable and therefore meaningful theory which does influence conduct. Such confusion of practical with ethical rules is often promoted by moralists. A mother trying to explain to her children why stealing is unethical finds it easy to explain that stealing does not pay, but impossible to explain why it is unethical. Even highly educated moralists often argue that ethical conduct is expedient.

The subject of a simple ethical doctrine may be meaningful even when the predicate is senseless, and the predicate may suggest or connote things it does not say. Thus the doctrine, "Stealing is unethical," has a meaningful subject, and the meaningless predicate may suggest that those who steal will be punished. Men who believe immoral conduct will be punished in heaven are rarely willing to leave punishment to heaven. Therefore, when they say some particular conduct is unethical they often clearly suggest that they plan to penalize or punish those who engage in such conduct. Such warnings are so obvious that most men listen carefully to the meaningless ethical theories supported by their neighbors.

It is never possible to enforce all ethical rules on all men in any area, but it is possible to make it pay to be at least nominally moral. Some ethical rules are enforced by law, some by social approval or disapproval, and some by discharging men from their jobs. Thus moral doctrines which are literally meaningless can greatly influence conduct. However, they would influence conduct in the same way if they were changed into meaningful factual statements that such and such conduct will be punished in certain ways.

Apologists for religion have often claimed that modern atheists and positivists are able to live in peace with each other because they practice the moral rules developed by religious leaders long after they repudiate religion. This argument assumes that moral rules are meaningful whereas they are in fact meaningless. Since they are meaningless, they can not guide the conduct of non-religious men. Such men are usually honest, industrious, friendly, etc., because they believe it pays, not because they believe it is moral. They can understand why honest men prosper; they cannot understand why honest men are moral. And the theory that honest men prosper is a scientific theory, not a moral theory, because it can be tested by observation and experiment. No revelation is needed to support it.

5. *Conscience and Duty*

Most priests and philosophers teach that every man has a conscience, a moral faculty that enables him to distinguish between right and wrong conduct by intuition or reason and which makes him feel remorseful or ashamed when he has done something unethical. This dogma is almost universally accepted today. Literature is full of stories about men who relied upon their conscience in making difficult decisions or who went against the clear advice of their conscience and afterwards felt conscience-stricken.

The first and most obvious objection to such theories about the conscience is that the term *conscience* has no observable referent or image, and is therefore meaningless. However, it is possible to use the adjective and adverbial forms of *conscience* meaningfully by defining them so as to describe specific kinds of observable conduct. For instance, we can say that a man acts conscientiously when he obeys certain rules of conduct.

In the last 50 years, psychologists and anthropologists have begun to study feelings of remorse and shame. They have discovered that the so-called dictates of conscience are determined by childhood training. For instance, if a child has been taught to go naked, he does not feel ashamed when naked, but if he has been taught to wear clothes, he feels ashamed when he does not wear them. In some primitive tribes and in some families in civilized countries, children are taught to steal and lie. Their "conscience" therefore tells them that it is right to do so. In other tribes, children are taught that head-hunting and cannibalism are proper. As a result, they feel conscience-stricken if they do not collect heads and eat human flesh.

Until recently, most Christian girls were taught that sexual relations are immoral before marriage and low and unclean after marriage. Consequently, they had strong guilt feelings about premarital relations and often were ashamed of normal sexual relations after marriage. Psychiatrists try to cure such cases by teaching women that sexual relations are normal and wholesome, but it is difficult to change the reactions men learn as children. Chiefly for this reason, a large proportion of married Christian women never learn to enjoy normal sexual relations even after marriage.

Closely related to the ethical doctrine that every man has a conscience which can tell him what conduct is morally right and what is wrong is the theory that men feel a sense of duty to do what is morally right. Our analysis of conscience applies to the sense of duty. Both are the result of childhood training, and such training can make men feel duty-bound to own slaves, eat human flesh, or kill their aged parents. On the other hand, parents and teachers can make men feel duty-bound to pick up trash in the street and to study political issues carefully before going to the polls. Scientific parents and educators of the future *will* continue to make men conscientious and dutiful, for utilitarian reasons, long after they have ceased to believe in the moral conscience, moral duties, and ethics.

6. *The Confusion of Ethics with Applied Science*

The term *ethics* has been used for 2500 years as a name for religious or philosophic theories concerning problems of personal conduct. These theories are now being gradually replaced by applied science. In order to deny or obscure this change, many religious and philosophic writers have included some applied science in ethics. In other words, they have claimed that some conduct is ethical because scientists can prove that it is expedient. We believe that this common claim is seriously confusing. To use the term *ethics* to denote the scientific treatment of problems of conduct is as misleading as to use the word *god* to describe the impersonal galaxies in which atheists believe. Yet there are many writers who mislead readers in both ways. We offer a few illustrations.

In his book *Moral Standards* (1949), C. H. Patterson wrote:

> Those who will not work do not deserve the same treatment as those who do work. To give it to them will not only encourage laziness . . . but will rob the others of a necessary incentive for doing their best work. (p. 418)

Deserve is a moral term. Scientists cannot prove that men deserve anything. The question of what kind and amount of wages maximizes output is a scientific question which belongs to economics or scientific management, not to ethics. There is no reason why it should be discussed in a book on "moral standards." However, since all moral questions are meaningless, the discussion of meaningful scientific problems like methods of wage payment in books on ethics helps to hide the fact that moral problems are both few and meaningless.

In his brilliant and lucid *History of Western Philosophy* (1945), Bertrand Russell asserted that:

> "The ethical, as opposed to the political [science] question is one as to sympathy. Sympathy, in the sense of being made unhappy by the suffering of others, is to some extent natural to human beings . . ." (p. 771)

But ethics tells when we *ought morally* to do something, not when we naturally feel sympathetic. The scientist, not the moralist, describes when we feel sympathetic and also why we feel sympathetic. Russell's quoted discussion of sympathy is a venture into scientific hypothesis, but he confuses it with ethics.

Still another example of the confusion of ethics with science is to be found in the theory that a new scientific ethics can be created by studying biological evolution. Herbert Spencer argued that ethics is the science of survival. Conduct that aids the individual, the group, or the species to survive is ethical. Conduct which does not is unethical. This makes all ethical principles verifiable. Why then should they be left to the moralist? Or, if verified by scientists, why should they be called ethics instead of science?

Prof. Ralph Barton Perry of Harvard has ably explained why we should use the scientific, rather than the religious or philosophic, method of solving problems of conduct

(*Realms of Value*, 1954). Unfortunately, he has obscured and weakened his arguments by redefining unscientific terms like *morality* and *value* and using them to state his major conclusions. For instance, he redefines *morality* as scientific rules of conduct and *value* as the quality possessed by anything men want. This permits him to claim that he is not attacking morality or values as such when in fact he rejects what these nouns have usually denoted.

C. *Aesthetics*

Philosophy includes at least two separate classes of theory concerning personal conduct—ethical theory and aesthetic theory. The moralist says that we should do what is ethical and the teacher of aesthetics says that we should create and/or enjoy beautiful things. Aesthetics is not merely a theory of what is beautiful. It is also in part a theory of personal conduct, of how men should create and react to beautiful things.

Due to the efforts of aesthetic philosophers, many teachers try to tell their students: (1) how to determine what is beautiful, (2) how to create beautiful things, and (3) how to enjoy beautiful things. For instance, teachers of English and other literature spend many hours trying to educate their students to distinguish between aesthetically good and bad books, to write aesthetically good books, and to enjoy the aesthetically best books (Shakespeare, Goethe, Moliere, etc.).

We have already explained in detail why moral theories are meaningless. The same analysis applies with little change to aesthetic theory. We shall therefore restate and apply this analysis very briefly.

An aethetic conclusion is deduced from rational premises obtained by intuition, but every student of aesthetics can, and many do, begin with different premises. Hence, even if their deductive reasoning is perfect, they usually arrive at different conclusions. These conclusions may be valid, but they have not been proven to be true. Indeed, since no method of verifying them can be conceived, they must be senseless.

When philosophers say an object is beautiful or aesthetically good, they do not mean that it is pleasant to read, observe, or study this object. Such statements are verifiable and therefore belong to science, specifically to psychology. And, after all, if men already enjoy beautiful objects, why waste time teaching them that they should enjoy them? University professors never bother to urge their men students to like pretty girls because this is unnecessary. However, they often try hard to teach them to like the works of Shakespeare, Beethoven, Leonardo da Vinci, etc.

Apologists for such teaching sometimes claim that while most students do not like aesthetically fine literature or art when they first encounter it, they can be taught to enjoy it. However, this claim is unverifiable and meaningless because we have no way to distinguish between aesthetically good and bad art. It may be possible to teach students to like the plays of Shakespeare, although we doubt it, but how can we prove that these plays are aesthetically good?

It is true that many critics have praised Shakespeare's plays, partly because they enjoy them and partly because they think this will induce people to accept them as competent critics. But a play is not aesthetically beautiful because it is liked or praised by high-brow critics, and what pleases one critic may not please another. A critic may be able to determine what plays are enjoyed by other highbrows. A public opinion poll could do the same. But no critic or public opinion poll can determine what is intrinsically beautiful.

D. The Scientific Treatment of Problems of Conduct

We turn now from the ethical and aesthetic to the scientific study and treatment of problems of personal conduct. The methods of treatment differ radically, and we shall try to explain how and why this is so.

Scientific work and scientific theories serve chiefly to help men solve personal problems. Pure science is useful because it can be used to develop principles of applied science, which can be used to solve such problems. Moreover, all personal problems are practical problems as to what conduct is most expedient, and applied science is the only means of solving them. Problems which cannot be solved by existing or conceivable applied science are senseless.

The scientific study and treatment of problems of human conduct can best be described and briefly explained by three major generalizations: (1) scientists assume that human acts are as fully determined by external causes as chemical reactions, (2) they assume that men already know what they wish to achieve and therefore they merely help them to achieve these given ends, and (3) all meaningful problems of human conduct can now or eventually be solved by some group of scientists. We shall now elaborate these points.

1. *Scientists Assume that Human Conduct is Determined*

Scientists assume that personal acts, like all other events, have observable causes. If they were not caused, scientific study of human conduct would be useless.

Scientists try to help men control events, including human acts. If these events had no cause, they would be uncontrollable. Personal advice, the laws of the state, and social reforms are all based upon the assumption that they can change conduct because conduct is caused or determined.

Parents, teachers, and rulers learned long ago that human conduct can be changed by example, by suggestions, by commands, by laws, by offering rewards, by threatening punishment, etc. Scientists have recently learned that many other things influence conduct. With further scientific progress we shall learn even more about the causes determining conduct. We shall never know all such causes perfectly, but this is equally true of the causes of chemical changes.

a. The Moral Doctrine of Freedom of the Will

The fact that personal decisions are at least partly determined by observable causes such as alcohol, head injuries, education, and parental behavior is now so obvious that even priests and philosophers concede it. Most of them still maintain, nevertheless, that the individual is either free to over-rule such influences by an act of free will or that his will creates new forces which compensate for the observable ones. In other words, they claim that, regardless of all observable factors, the individual is free to act as he pleases.

This doctrine, usually called freedom of the will, is inconsistent with determinism, and that is why most moralists reject determinism. However, it is easy to rephrase the freedom-of-the-will doctrine so as to make it consistent with determinism. That is one reason why many scientists claim to believe in freedom of the will. Here, as so often elsewhere, an analysis of the meaning of words is essential both to reveal meaningless problems and theories and to clarify meaningful theories.

To begin with, the nouns *freedom* and *will* are both nonsensical because they have no sensible referents. However, those who claim to believe in freedom of the will may intend to say that they believe men are free to act as they wish. We shall therefore analyze this statement.

The theory that men are free to act as they wish is vague and ambiguous because the adjective *free* is ambiguous. We say a man is free when he is out of jail, or when he is not a slave. We say he acts freely when he is not ordered or coerced to do what he does not wish to do. We also say he decides freely to do what he is required to do.

These illustrations suggest that the adjective *free* can be defined meaningfully, but it can also be meaningless. The test is whether a statement containing it is theoretically verifiable. Those who believe that men are free to act as they please have never been able to agree on how this theory could be verified. Until they do, the doctrine is meaningless.

Most men believe in freedom of the will because they feel free to do many things. But the ethical theory that men *are* free to act as they please is entirely distinct from the verifiable theory that men *feel* free to act as they please, within limits. Undoubtedly, men do normally feel free to do what they wish to do and are able to do. There is no contradiction betwen this fact and the theory of determinism. To reconcile them, it is only necessary to assume that the causes which determine conduct also determine what one wishes to do. Moreover, this assumption can easily be shown to be true in many cases. For instance, propaganda which determines conduct also determines what men want to do.

Critics of human determinism often identify it with fatalism. This is plausible because *fatalism* can be defined as synonymous with *determinism*, but it is also misleading because *fatalism* has other and more common senses which directly conflict with our definition of determinism. For instance, we say a man is a fatalist if he thinks it is impossible for men to influence their fate by acting wisely. In sharp contrast, the determinist knows that if men do the (scientifically) right thing, then as an inevitable result their fate will be improved. For him science serves chiefly to help men determine their own fate. This obvious difference between popular fatalism and scientific determinism is frequently overlooked by critics of determinism.

Probably the most common and influential argument for the doctrine of "freedom of the will" is the argument that this belief is essential to a moral life. But denial of this doctrine does not seem to affect personal conduct. Many religious sects, like the Calvinists, have denied freedom of the will, and their behavior does not appear to have been corrupted thereby. They did not act more lawlessly, more improvidently, or more brutally than their neighbors. Such conduct is of course inexpedient rather than immoral, but it is such conduct which is alleged to result from a denial of freedom of the will.

If personal conduct is completely determined, we ought not to blame ourselves or others for past mistakes. It is helpful to find out what past acts were *causally* responsible for later results, but it is useless and meaningless to try to discover who was "morally" responsible for past mistakes or anti-social acts. Both self-castigation and retaliatory punishment of others for such acts are pointless and harmful.

One of the many paradoxes of ethics is that most of those who urge us to love and forgive our fellow men also justify vindictive retaliatory punishment of immoral persons. They are led to this harsh conclusion by their interpretation of the theory of moral freedom. If men deliberately and freely choose to act wrongly, retaliation seems justified, regardless of its effect of future behavior. The scientific conclusion drawn from determinism is quite different. The scientist condemns for practical reasons both self-blame and vengence on wrong-doers. If he approves punishment, it is carefully designed to improve future conduct. He does not believe that some persons are morally guilty, that they should be morally blamed, that they should expiate their sins, that they should feel ashamed, etc. On the other hand, he believes that those who cause special costs should usually be required to pay them in order to permit men to balance the benefits against the costs of each action. If men are unable to balance gains against costs, and therefore repeatedly incur costs or cause damage they cannot pay for, they should be confined in institutions for the sick, the feeble-minded, and the insane. But no effort to prove them morally guilty or to make them feel ashamed should be made.

b. Pseudo-Scientific Arguments Against Determinism

Modern defenders of freedom of the will sometimes argue that recent developments in physics have disproven the old scientific assumption of determinism. This is not a new argument. When Galileo first taught that a moving object continues to move ahead equally fast until something slows it down or deflects it, he was accused of denying determinism. Earlier thinkers had thought that continued movement requires a continuing cause or force, and, when Galileo denied this, his critics thought he was denying that movement is caused. This suggests that a new scientific theory may seem to deny causation merely because it contradicts an old theory as to the cause of particular events.

Heisenberg's theory that it is impossible to determine simultaneously both where an electron is and how fast it is moving, because the measurement of one distorts the other, has been named the principle of indeterminacy. This ambiguous title has caused many religious thinkers (J. W. N. Sullivan, Eddington, and Jeans) to claim that this theory disproves the doctrine of scientific determinism. But the fact that we cannot simultaneously determine (observe or measure) two things does not prove they are not determined (caused) by observable causes. *Determined* is used in two different senses in this argument, and the same thing may therefore be determined and indeterminable.

Some writers try to refute the theory of determinism

by appealing to the modern doctrine that certain scientific principles are statistical. They often cite those concerning the behavior of gas particles, and argue that since we cannot predict the behavior of each particle, determinism has been disproven. However, the fact that we do not now have enough information to predict behavior does not prove that this behavior is undetermined. Only a person who is very eager to arrive at the latter conclusion could think it did.

It is sometimes claimed that human conduct cannot be completely determined because it is purposive, i.e., is influenced by future goals—a kind of causation not found in the inanimate world. However, future events cannot directly affect current events. It is current thinking about future events or results which affects present conduct. The fact that animals can anticipate the results of their actions is not only consistent with the theory of scientific determinism but is indeed dependant upont it. When men plan to achieve future results, they assume that their actions will determine future events.

2. *The Scientist Helps Men Achieve Given Ends*

The assumption that all personal conduct is determined, and therefore controllable by applied scientific means, is the first basic doctrine which distinguishes the scientific from the moralistic student of conduct. The second, which we shall now discuss, is the doctrine that men already know what they want to achieve as ends and that therefore the scientist can and should strive solely to advise them concerning the means to these ends.

a. Men Know What Ends They Want to Achieve

Theologians and philosophers have long taught that science is purely descriptive and that consequently men must rely on the moralist for prescriptive advice on personal conduct. In sharp contrast, the scientist believes that men already know what they want to achieve as ends and that therefore any advice as to what men ought to want to achieve is superfluous as well as senseless.

It has long been customary for scientists to explain that what men are, what they want, and what they do is determined by heredity and environment. Heredity here denotes the long process of evolution, not a mysterious force, and environment includes all things observed or experienced by men now living.

The study of what men instinctively and/or constitutionally want to achieve is a vital part of current psychological research. Psychologists have prepared tentative lists of such ends, but are far from complete agreement. However, this does not affect our present argument. All that is essential to our argument is the generally accepted scientific principle that millions of years of struggle for survival has resulted in the survival of men fitted to survive. They are fitted to survive because among other things they instinctively or constitutionally try to remain alive and to have frequent sexual relaxations. These are the ultimate unchangeable ends of all men. To achieve these ends is relatively or absolutely pleasant.

While both personal survival and sexual intercourse are ultimate human ends which it is futile to condemn, they may occasionally be inconsistent with each other. Conduct which achieves more frequent or more satisfying sexual intercourse, for instance with a neighbor's wife, may shorten one's life. Conversely, it may be necessary to endure being separated from women in order to remain alive. Scientists can tell men how their ends conflict and advise them as to the effects of seeking one end by a given means upon their achievement of the other end, but they cannot meaningfully approve or disapprove either end.

Evolution has produced men with intermediate as well as ultimate ends. They constitutionally dislike and avoid many dangerous experiences and certain poisonous or injurious foods, gases, objects, etc. They naturally like beautiful healthy women more than homely sickly women because the former can have more children and these children will be more likely to survive and procreate. A great many means to personal survival and sexual success are themselves constitutionally pleasant, and many experiences which hamper or prevent the achievement of these ends are naturally unpleasant or painful. Thus all men desire to be healthy, sexually attractive, skillful, wise, wealthy, powerful, loved, honored, etc., both because to be so aids survival and sexual success and because it is pleasant.

Intermediate ends are inconsistent with each other much more frequently than the two ultimate ends. Hours spent becoming wise cannot also be used fully to become healthy or wealthy. Hence, the scientist can help men to fare well by explaining why, where, and how far such ends conflict, and what means may be used to reconcile them. But it would be senseless for him to claim that one should try to achieve one end more than another because it is intrinsically or morally better. Only the individual can compare one end with another and feel directly which attracts him the most. There is no other sensible method of comparing ends.

While men constitutionally desire or find it pleasant to achieve all ultimate and some intermediate ends, how intensely they strive for any of these ends is affected by education and legislation. Teachers and law-makers can reward or penalize the achievement of any end, and thus make it more or less desired. By promising sufficient rewards and penalties, they can even persuade soldiers to die for their country and martyrs to die for professing unpopular views. This does not prove that men want to die, but that they are willing to die in order to become famous, to avoid becoming infamous, to benefit their families, etc. Men who commit suicide without promise of reward or penalty do so to avoid painful experiences, not because they instinctively want to die.

The fact that men are so constituted that they want to achieve certain ends, by pleasant rather than unpleasant means when possible, is demonstrable and vitally significant. To deny it is unrealistic. To approve it is superfluous. However, psychiatrists have learned that when we help men to become what they naturally enjoy becoming—healthy, popular, etc.,—we make men more lawabiding, more peaceful, more productive, etc. In other words, when men are able to achieve what they constitutionally enjoy achieving, they become more industrious workers, more considerate husbands, more loving fathers, and better citizens. Conversely, the enforcement of moral rules is often, if not usually, harmful because it makes it more difficult for men to achieve the ends they naturally wish to achieve. And when these rules are beneficial, they are identical with applied science and hence superfluous.

Since all constitutional human ends are the product of evolution, it is possible to change them by eugenic measures, i.e., by controlled evolution. We could even breed men who would commit suicide far more often and have sexual relations far less often than modern men.

It is also possible to breed men who can achieve more easily the ends which normal men now have. We could breed men who would be more resistant to disease germs, more intelligent, more loving, more cooperative, etc. Indeed, in advanced states, eugenic reform is the most promising of all scientific methods for making men healthier and happier. Rich men are often less healthy and happy than poor men because they are constitutionally inferior.

All ultimate, and some intermediate, human ends are instinctive or constitutional, but experience and education partly determine how intensely and by what means men strive to achieve constitutional ends. Moreover, they create many artificial intermediate ends. For instance men learn that in order to marry attractive women, raise large families, and live long and pleasantly, they should try to become wise and/or rich. Most specific human actions are directed towards the achievement of such learned goals, but these goals appeal to men only when they seem to be steps toward the achievement of unlearned goals, goals which attract all men because men are men.

We have noted that scientists can evaluate men, according to the intermediate instinctive or constitutional ends they seek, and can then recommend eugenic measures to breed out certain classes of men. They can also evaluate men according to the acquired or cultural ends they seek on the basis of how well these artificial ends serve ultimate instinctive ends, survival of the individual and the species. They can then advise parents and teachers to train children differently, i.e., so that they will seek acquired ends which serve ultimate constitutional ends more effectively. Thus scientists can help both to breed and to train men who would want to do things which few or no living men now want to do. In the meantime, however, they should seek only to help men do what they now want to do. In other words, scientists, like other men, should do only what it is now expedient to do. And when we say "should," we mean only that it is expedient to act so.

It may be some time before a radical eugenic program is politically feasible. In the meantime, very great changes in what men want as intermediate cultural ends may be quickly achieved by education, by advertising, by raising real incomes, and by other changes in environmental factors. During the past century there have been many reforms in education, and these have already changed what men want as means. Advertising has also greatly influenced many men. We believe that eventually advertising will be used to help consumers make wise choices, not to persuade them to buy from X rather than from Y, or to buy things they do not need. There are many ways of changing what men want by giving them better information concerning economic goods and the effects of consuming them. This requires applied science, not ethics.

It is important to note that, while different men can want different things, this does not imply that they disagree about what they want. If A wants to kill his enemies and B wants to be kind to them, A and B do not disagree, they merely differ. Men can disagree over statements of facts or theories, not over what each likes or wants. Scientists can help to determine which statement is true, and therefore who is right, when men disagree about factual statements, but they cannot determine who is right when men want or enjoy different things. Moralists, of course, claim that they can determine what men ought to want, and often speak of disagreements over goals, but their claims are nonsensical.

If A wants B to do something and B does not want to do it, they may seem to disagree, but in fact they may agree completely. Both may recognize that if B does what A desires it will benefit A and injure B, and if they disagree on this, the issue is factual and can be decided by scientists. It is not a disagreement over what A and B want but over the results of certain conduct.

It may also appear that men can disagree about what they want when they must act together or through a representative. Men clearly do disagree as to what government policies are wise. But in such cases they are disagreeing over theories as to what will benefit them or they are recognizing that a policy which benefits A will harm B. They are not disagreeing about what A or B individually wants and enjoys.

b. The Scientist Prescribes Means, not Ends

While the consistent scientist does not prescribe the ends that men should desire, he does prescribe the means that should be used to achieve desired ends. All applied science can be stated as prescriptions concerning personal conduct. Thus a doctor may tell his patients that in order to stay well they should avoid close contact with tubercular and syphilitic persons. Such advice is prescriptive and scientific, not ethical, even when it prescribes conduct approved by moralists. To do something in order to be healthy is quite different from doing something in order to be moral.

Philosophers frequently claim that ethics is prescriptive while science is descriptive, and many scientists influenced by philosophy have accepted and restated this claim. This claim is plausible only because it is ambiguous.

Every ethical doctrine can be stated in a descriptive form. For instance, the rule, "Do not steal," can be restated as, "To steal is unethical." This implies that one should not steal, but the descriptive scientific theory, "Fire burns painfully," also implies than one should not touch fire. It is true of course that descriptive ethical statements are meaningless, whereas descriptive scientific statements are meaningful, but prescriptive ethical doctrines are equally senseless. Hence, there is no good reason to call ethics more prescriptive than science.

The theory that science is or should be purely descriptive has proved useful to conservatives. It implies that social scientists are being unscientific when they propose social reforms like health insurance. If science is purely descriptive, it is impossible to prove scientifically that any political reform will probably be beneficial. In the absence of such proof, there can be no good reason for reform of any kind. Hence, most conservatives want to and do believe that social science should be purely descriptive. They influence very strongly the social science taught in our universities.

Scientists tell men what means are most expedient to achieve given ends. Men who are proud of their morality frequently assert that they act upon principle and not from considerations of expediency or self-interest. However, principles of conduct may be moral or scientific. The former are senseless, the latter sensible. Thus moral men act upon senseless principles; scientists upon sensible principles. And acting upon sensible principles is doing what is expedient.

When moral rules prescribe means, such as honest conduct, as ends in themselves, they make it impossible to suit the means to the ends. This is one of the chief errors of moralists. They have taken over many rules which it is usually, but not always, expedient to apply and have turned them into absolute universal rules which must always be applied. This makes intelligent choice of means impossible for moral persons.

The chief contribution of Machiavelli to political science was the theory that rulers should do what is expedient even when it is called immoral. But he failed to explain that such cases are a minority and that many moral rules endorse conduct which is usually expedient. His critics have made a similar mistake. They also assume that what is expedient is usually called immoral and have therefore concluded that Michiavellian policies are usually immoral.

3. *All Conduct Problems Should be Solved Scientifically*

We have explained that: (1) scientists assume that all human conduct is determined, in other words that such conduct is understandable and controllable, and (2) they merely help men to achieve more easily what they already wish to achieve. We shall now explain and illustrate the third basic generalization concerning the scientific treatment of problems of personal conduct, namely the principle that all meaningful problems of conduct can and should be solved by scientific reasoning.

Problems of personal conduct may be divided into two classes: (1) private problems, those which can be solved by individual action and (2) social problems, those which can be solved only by social or cooperative action.

Private problems should be solved by the use of the applied sciences which deal with them—personal hygiene, medicine, vocational guidance, marriage counseling, psychiatry, etc. Social problems should be treated by the application of the social sciences. All meaningful problems of human conduct can and should be studied by some group of applied scientists.

Most moralists can state their entire theory of ethics and many of its applications in a single volume. To state all scientific theories which can be applied to problems of conduct would require thousands of volumes. Nearly all scientific theories are now useful in this way, and the rest soon will be.

a. Private Problems

In order to solve his private problems, the individual should try to get as good a general and vocational education as he can afford and understand and he should consult professional advisors (doctors, lawyers, psychiatrists, etc.) whenever their advice is worth its cost. With the steady growth of science, education and professional advice are constantly becoming more helpful.

It is unnecessary to urge the individual to try to solve his personal problems, i.e., to seek to do what he already wants to do. However, it is possible to help him solve his problems by giving him more education and more professional advice.

The great majority of voters believe that many problems of conduct, the so-called moral problems, should be studied and solved by religious moralists rather than by applied scientists. Religion is not supposed to be taught in American public schools. Moreover, many applied sciences are very new. Hence, most public school teachers have only recently begun to teach their students how to solve some of the most important problems of private conduct. And the private school teachers who have long discussed such problems have usually merely repeated meaningless moral dogmas.

Young people badly need instruction in the practical application of the specialized sciences to common personal problems. In recent years, some progress has been made in introducing courses in personal hygiene, diet, vocational guidance, etc., but these courses are still uncommon and cover only a few of the major personal problems. Teenagers need to learn why it pays to be honest, industrious, and thrifty, how to make friends and influence people, how to select a mate, how to achieve wholesome and satisfying sex relations, how to choose a vocation and find a job, etc., etc.

b. Social Problems

As we have noted, all social problems should be studied by social scientists. In order to solve such problems, voters and rulers need education in the social sciences and history and the constant advice of experts who have specialized on individual social problems (tariff experts, taxation experts, sanitation experts, zoning experts, etc.) They do not need, and in fact are usually injured by, advice from priests, philosophers, and moralists.

It is unnecessary to urge voters and rulers to solve social problems for ethical reasons since the solution of such problems would benefit them. Intelligent voting on tariffs, sanitation, defense, etc., makes most voters healthier, wealthier, safer, etc. Measures which injure a minority but benefit a majority of voters will be approved by the majority, assuming adequate education. When voters vote unwisely, they need to become better informed, not to be morally exhorted. It is impossible to vote immorally because *immoral* is meaningless.

When a man solves a personal problem intelligently, his conduct may injure other men more than it benefits him.

How to minimize such anti-social conduct, whether deliberate or not, is always a social problem. The best way to prevent or reduce anti-social conduct is to create artificial penalties for it. Such penalties should serve, not to punish men for crimes committed, but to make crime unprofitable or inexpedient.

It is also wise to reward men whenever they do something which benefits other persons. This is largely an economic problem, but there are non-economic rewards (medals, titles, uniforms, etc.,) which should be used. How to determine and apply such penalties and rewards is one of the chief problems of social science. In an ideal society, all socially desirable conduct would be expedient, and all anti-social conduct would be unprofitable and therefore would occur only when men are misinformed.

In primitive human societies, anti-social conduct is common because rulers have not learned what conduct is anti-social, because they have not announced the proper rewards and penalties, and because they cannot enforce the penalties they have announced. As states become larger, more heterogeneous, and more advanced, criminal laws improve, but it becomes more difficult to catch law-breakers. Rulers become wiser and stronger, but anti-social conduct becomes easier and safer.

Since it is difficult to enforce laws against anti-social acts, rulers long ago called upon priests and philosophers to threaten law-breakers with supernatural rewards and punishment. They hoped that men who do not fear visible police and courts would fear invisible police and courts. And theologians did their best to help rulers enforce the laws. In return for this service, rulers have nearly always supported religion. That is why modern revolutionary movements have often attacked the priests as well as the rulers.

However, the use of scientific means (rewards and penalties) to influence personal conduct is even older. It has been practiced in human families from the beginning of human family life, and there is some evidence that lower animals also use it in training their young. Naive applied science is far older than ethics as a means of controlling personal conduct.

We have noted that ethical statements influence conduct chiefly because they imply, but do not say, that certain conduct will be rewarded or punished. Perhaps the chief reason that ethical statements often fail to influence conduct is that they are frequently made by men who cannot appreciably reward or penalize their hearers. For instance, a modern American preacher in a large city who tells his congregation that it is immoral to be a heretic, influences the conduct of his hearers little if any. They know that he cannot significantly penalize them for becoming heretical. During the Inquisition, by contrast, such moral statements affected conduct very greatly because priests were able to burn heretics at the stake, and did burn or imprison millions of them.

Political economy is the oldest and most advanced science dealing with social problems of conduct. It was the first social study whose leaders abandoned or ignored ethics and became relatively scientific in dealing with social problems. Since Adam Smith, most economists have observed what men want instead of telling them what they ought morally to want. They have largely restricted themselves to prescribing how men can achieve their given ends in the most economical, i.e., expedient, way. Hence, political economy illustrates the scientific treatment of social problems of conduct. For instance, it suggests that the ideal way to encourage desired conduct and discourage anti-social conduct is to reward the former and penalize the latter.

The chief problem which social scientists must solve is how to decide which social policies are most beneficial, i.e., which policies help men to achieve most completely what they already individually desire to do. Every social action affects different men differently. It benefits some and injures others, and those who are benefited or injured are unequally affected. For instance, prohibition injured brewers and saloon keepers, but it also benefited many people.

Economists have developed a method of analysis which enables them to measure how much different men have been benefited or injured by a given social act. They measure, or allow individuals to measure, these effects in a common denominator, money, add up the resulting valuations, and subtract the total value of costs from that of benefits. The social policy which yields the largest net positive difference is the most beneficial.

We shall call such calculation *economic analysis* because it has been developed by economists for the solution of economic problems. However, it is also suitable for the solution of non-economic social problems. In fact, it is the only method which can be used to solve them scientifically. Political scientists, sociologists, historians, and other non-economic social scientists have never created any alternative method of scientifically evaluating social policies and never will. They can be unscientific and try to consider the unmeasurable moral consequences of social policies, and they can improve traditional methods of economic analysis, but they cannot evaluate political and social policies scientifically without measuring and comparing their effects upon different individuals in some common denominator, i.e., in money. Thus economic analysis is far more important than economists have claimed it to be.

Bertrand Russell once asserted that ethics alone can deal with cases in which what one man wants conflicts with what another man wants. This is a gross error. Most such problems are economic problems which economists alone can solve. And many non-economic social problems also can be solved by economic analysis.

While the study of economic problems has been dominated for 200 years be relatively scientific thinkers, there has been a minor anti-scientific reaction in the last generation. The leaders of this reaction assert that science is purely descriptive, and that therefore social scientists should never recommend the application of social science to the solution of private and social problems. They claim that all such problems are ethical problems, and so can not be solved by scientists. They want some priests or philosopher to be the final authority in such matters. Good illustrations of this doctrine may be found in the attacks of economists like Lionel Robbins and I. M. D. Little on welfare economics. For instance, Little claims that "Welfare economics and ethics cannot . . . be separated" and that therefore scientists cannot solve problems of economic conduct. This is, of course, the only position consistent with religion and philosophy. Economists who use science to suggest economic reforms and remain religious or philosophic are completely inconsistent. No compromise between these points of view is reasonable.

Economists define *economic value* as the rate of exchange between one good and another. The exchange rate with money is called *price,* and price theory is the most important part of value theory. Economic goods are defined as valuable goods. They are valued or desired by men.

Some moralists have used the term *value* to denote anything which is valued. This turns most economic values into ethical values, and implies that moralists can solve, or help to solve, most economic problems. It is a bad definition of *ethical value* because it makes the term meaningful and therefore turns ethical problems into scientific problems. Ethical value theory is senseless. It deals with what men ought to want as ethical end-in-themselves, not with the sensible problem of what they already want. Economic value theory is meaningful, ethical value theory is not. It is especially unfortunate, therefore, that Little and other economists often use the term *value* to describe alleged ethical values in discussions of economic values.

While political economy has been basically scientific for almost 200 years, political science, a much newer study, remains relatively unscientific. It should be called political philosophy, not political science. Thus most political scientists still teach that the function of political theory is to help men achieve ethical goals, not to help them survive and procreate. Some of them believe that the state is a divine institution and others think it has a metaphysical existence separate from that of the country and the people. Many still believe that the individual has certain metaphysical natural rights which the state should not restrict. The philosophic theory of a social contract among citizens also continues to be influential. One of the major traditional problems of this "sciencc" is that concerning the exact metaphysical nature and location of sovereignty. Even the most advanced political thinkers have scarcely gotten beyond the doctrine that men have an ethical duty to do what is in the interest of the largest number of people. It will be some time before the majority of political theorists realize that political science should merely aid men to do what they already want to do, and that the problem of whether what they want to do is ethical is nonsensical.

Since all private and social problems should be solved by scientists rather than by moralists, we ought to spend far more money on scientific research than we now do. Conversely, the great increase in expenditures upon scientific research in recent decades suggests that men are slowly but surely ceasing to believe in ethics and morality and are becoming more and more convinced that applied science is useful in solving problems of conduct. Probably there is no better index of the effect of positivists on private and social conduct than the percentage of national income spent upon scientific research on psychological and social problems We recommend and confidently expect a 1000% increase in this percentage for the world as a whole within 50 to 100 years.

E. The Application of Science to Problems of Conduct

We have explained that all problems of personal and political conduct should be studied by some group of scientists and that all applied science applies to problems of conduct. To repeat what scientists have prescribed as intelligent conduct would therefore require a summary of all applied science. We cannot even offer a summary of such a summary here, but we can illustrate the application of science to problems of conduct by a few examples.

We begin with the general problem of how to prevent crime because so many people are interested in it. This may be divided into two main parts, the problem of how to prevent events which cause or facilitate crime and the problem of how to catch and penalize criminals.

Among the chief events which cause men to commit crimes are poor education, association with criminals, vain attempts to find work, uninsured sickness, excessive gambling, the use of money for large purchases, etc. The social scientist believes that it is possible to eliminate some of these events completely and to make others far less frequent. He advocates better education, segregation of first offenders in jail, full employment, insurance against sickness and accidents, etc. We believe that the use of specie or paper money to pay for things costing more than perhaps $5.00 should be prohibited. If all such payments were made by check, there would be few large stocks of cash to steal, and stolen cash could not be used to pay rent or taxes or to buy goods costing over $5.00. Many other scientific methods of removing the causes of crime and making crime more difficult have been developed by scientists or will soon be developed.

We turn to the problem of catching criminals. The authors of mystery books have publicized many new scientific methods of catching and convicting criminals, but most police are unable or unwilling to use these methods. For instance, lie detectors ought to be universally used and their results should be accepted as evidence in court. Moreover, all citizens should be photographed and fingerprinted, and both local and national police files should contain the results and must other information (address, signature, handwriting sample, criminal record, etc.) on all citizens. The government should also require that a sample bullet be fired from every pistol before it is sold, and that the name of the buyer be recorded, so that all bullets found at the place of any crime can be identified as coming from a specific person. We could suggest many other improved scientific measures of catching criminals, and we are confident of unlimited progress in the application of science to this problem.

Instead of using scientific lie detectors, we now use religious oaths to induce men to speak truthfully. So far as we are aware, no scientific experiments have ever been made to determine the effect of oath-taking upon truth-telling. Indeed, the mere suggestion of such experiments will probably be denounced as blasphemous by theologians. Yet perjury under oath is very common, and nearly all convicted perjurors are religious men. By contrast, critics of the lie detector often condemn it because it has been scientifically proven that it does not yield correct results in all cases.

The fact that there is no evidence that religious oaths are effective is not the only argument *against* using them. Their use requires many men who are not religious to affirm implicitly belief in a deity. Thus oaths against perjury make some men perjure themselves implicitly. This is often humiliating to non-believers.

For our second illustration of the application of science to personal conduct we shall discuss an entirely different kind of problem, that of selecting a mate. This problem has as yet been little studied by scientists but they have already created some useful theories. For instance, biologists have learned that certain kinds of marriages are apt to result in defective children and miscarriages. All young people ought to have such information before they decide to marry, perhaps even before they decide to go together.

Psychologists and psychiatrists have also developed some valuable theories as to which married couples are most likely to be happy. Thus they have learned that people who choose mates with similar educational records are more apt to be happy than those who do not. All such information should be given young people in high school.

Most important of all, we should spend billions of dollars on scientific research to learn more about how to select a mate wisely. Here as elsewhere we are still in the earliest stages of scientific thinking.

For our third and final illustration of the application of science to conduct, let us consider the problem of how many children to have after marriage. Most moralists have always taught that men and women should do nothing to prevent the birth of unwanted children. The scientific solution of this problem is to help parents to have as many or as few children as they desire. Scientists have created many means for controlling conception and pregnancy. As a result, most enlightened parents in advanced countries are now relatively free to have as few or as many children as they desire. This is one of the greatest achievements of modern scientists.

Scientific methods of controlling conception are being rapidly improved. In a few decades we shall probably be able to make ourselves sterile for any desired period by swallowing harmless and inexpensive pills. Moreover, birth control will eventually become as common in China and India as in the United States. This will help solve many serious problems in these countries.

It is worth noting that political authorities will soon be able to control the growth of population in any country without regulating the marital relations of any couple. This will be achieved by offering monetary rewards for desired births and monetary penalties for undesired births. Parents will remain free to balance what they gain against what they lose by having an additional child. Such balancing is a part of all intelligent decision-making.

F. Cultural Relativity

The scientific theory of personal conduct which we have supported in this chapter is quite different from cultural relativity, the doctrine that any culture, i.e., any set of customs and institutions, is as valid or good as any other. This point deserves to be emphasized because many anthropologists and sociologists have accepted the theory of cultural relativity or relativism and have defended it as *the* scientific evaluation of different ways of living.

It is true that all ethical theories are meaningless, but it is not true that different cultures are equally productive, satisfying, or intelligent. And it is meaningless to speak of customs as *valid.* Only a statement can be valid. Social customs can be more or less backward or advanced, they can result in more or less slums, war, and disease, but they cannot be logically valid or ethically good.

A consistent social scientist does not regard backward and advanced peoples as equally successful or intelligent. He tries to classify tribes and nations according to their degree of cultural development. He is eager to obtain statistics on the death rates, education, wealth, and industry of different peoples because he regards such data as useful and significant. And he uses such information to evaluate customs and institutions. His evaluations are meaningful and scientific, not meaningless and ethical. They are judgments which men can use to improve their customs and institutions. It follows that the doctrine of cultural relativity is unscientific.

G. *Arguments Against the Scientific Treatment of Problems of Conduct*

Many arguments against the positivist thesis that problems of personal and social conduct can be solved only by scientists have been advanced. We have already answered some of them, notably in our general defense of science, but we shall now briefly discuss a few more.

Some who deny that the scientific method is applicable to social problems are using very narrow definitions of scientific method. They assume, usually without so stating, that the scientific method requires experiments. This is an unjustified assumption. Geology and astronomy, for instance, are based largely upon the observation of uncontrolled events or results.

Moreover, there are almost unlimited opportunities for social experiments under partly controlled conditions. Some of these, such as experiments on the effect of propaganda on elections, can be performed by individual scientists with adequate funds. Others require the consent of the voters, but this consent will become steadily easier to secure as more and more voters learn to understand scientific methods.

Many social scientists use and praise what they call the historical approach to social problems without explaining that this is a scientific method. Prof. E. M. Sait, a political scientist, has explicitly stated it as an alternative to the scientific approach to political problems (*Political Institutions,* 1938, pp. 46-54). But history should be, and is steadily becoming, a summary of numerous individual reports of scientific observations. And theories based upon verifiable reports of observation of uncontrolled past events are just as scientific as theories based upon verifiable reports of controlled events or experiments.

It is sometimes implied that the conclusions arrived at by social scientists are not scientific because they are not certain. But certain conclusions are a result of religious or philosophic reasoning, not of scientific research. Even if a conclusion is only 51% probable, it is a scientific truth. Whenever we have more reason to accept than to deny a proposition we have scientific knowledge. And social scientists have already discovered many such probable truths. These truths are scientific truths because the claim that they are probably true can be verified.

C. H. Patterson charges that the scientific theory of conduct, which he called "relativism," "is inconsistent because it claims there are no universal principles of morality and at the same time it insists that everyone should accept relativism as true" *(Moral Standards,* p. 42). But a scientist does not say that men should accept scientific truth, using *should* as a moral term. If he uses *should,* he uses it quite differently. He means that if men use applied science, they will achieve desired, not ethical, results more easily.

In restating this argument, Patterson accuses the "relativist" of making "all moral judgments, including his own, meaningless" (p. 42). In fact, however, the consistent scientist does not make any moral judgments. And, when he discusses problems of conduct, he talks sense because his statements are verifiable.

C. I. Lewis has stated the same argument in different words. He claims that those who deny "value-apprehensions" resemble a Cretan who says that all Cretans are liars *(An Analysis of Knowledge and Valuation* 1946, p. 373). This implies that a denial of "value-apprehensions" is itself a value-apprehension, which is not true. Logic and ethics are quite different. Moreover, positivists do not deny value-apprehensions (moral theories); they merely assert that they are meaningless. Finally, it is *proper* for a Cretan to say that all Cretans are liars. The apparent contradiction is due to the unjustified assumption that such statements apply to themselves (see p. 17 above).

Barrows Dunham has asserted that the result of holding "moral judgments to be capable of no proof," i.e. meaningless, is that "one cannot rationally choose (i.e., choose on the basis of argument) between death camps and liberation" (*Man Against Myth,* p. 253). This argument ignores the fact that moral judgments differ radically from scientific judgments. It is plausible only because it is ambiguous. When he says "rationally choose," does he mean choose morally or scientifically? We have already noted that philosophy, and therefore philosophic ethics, is "rational," i.e. based upon rational intuition and rational deduction. That is why its conclusions are false or meaningless. On the other hand, scientific reasoning is also rational in a different sense, and scientific judgments of, i.e., rational choices between, such things as "death camps and liberation" are not only possible but commonplace.

When rephrased unambiguously, Dunham's argument claims that the result of holding moral judgments to be unprovable is that one should not choose *morally* between alternative means, but this conclusion does not mean we cannot choose *scientifically*. Many arguments against positivism turn out to be irrelevant when thus restated in an unambiguous way.

Some critics of positivism claim that when positivists reject ethics and/or morality they are attacking honest, law-abiding, and friendly behavior and approving their opposites. This criticism is plausible to many because ethics and morality are very ambiguous terms. Sometimes they refer to acts and sometimes to theories. *We must emphasize, therefore, that we have rejected theories of ethics and morality, not acts called moral or ethical. For instance, positivists do not disapprove of honest behavior, but they do disap-*

prove of all religious and philosophic theories as to why men should be honest. They believe that rejection of these meaningless theories and scientific study of the results of honest behavior would increase rather than decrease such behavior. They are convinced that it usually pays well to be honest, friendly, industrious, thrifty, studious, helpful, abstemious, etc., etc.

H. Conclusion

Men reason only in order to act more wisely. The only way to tell whether one personal act is wiser than another is to observe its consequences. The men who do this are applied scientists. Moralists, who rely on revelation and/or rational intuition, cannot help men to act wisely because they ignore the consequences of behavior. If they studied these consequences, they would become applied scientists and would find moral theory superfluous.

All personal conduct has consequences. All of it should be studied by pure and applied scientists in order to help men achieve desired results and avoid undesired results.

There are no problems of personal conduct which should be assigned to moralists. If scientists cannot yet solve certain problems of conduct, no one else can.

All moral problems and theories are superfluous or senseless. If they duplicate scientific problems and theories, they are superfluous. If they do not, they are senseless.

Men do not need moralists to tell them what ends they should seek. As a result of evolution, they nearly all want to continue living, to marry, and to raise children. As a result of education, they want to do these things thus and so. Since men already have ends, scientists can help them only by advising them how to achieve these desired ends more efficiently. But this is a very important task. All social progress consists of improvement in the means used to achieve instinctive or constitutional human ends.

Moralists continue to be numerous and influential because they defend old or new theories which men want to believe and cannot verify and because few men can detect the errors in moral reasoning. However, applied science is slowly but steadily replacing moral principles, especially among educated men. This important trend will probably continue until the majority of educated men in every country become completely scientific in their reasoning about all problems of personal conduct.

In 1930 we spent about 166 million dollars on scientific research. In 1956 we spent 6,000 millions. The author predicts that Americans will spend over 50,000 million dollars a year on such research by the year 2,000, assuming no further price inflation.

In 1900 there were five to ten times as many clergymen as scientists (full-time teachers of social and natural science, plus paid research scientists) in this country. By 1950 there were almost equal numbers of clergymen and scientists. We predict that by the year 2000 there will be five to ten times as many scientists as clergymen. This should greatly increase scientific thinking about problems of personal and social conduct.

Readable Books on Logical Positivism

*(*Designates most important)*

*Ayer, A. J., *Language, Truth and Logic,* (1936), 2nd ed., Gollancz, London, 1946.

Bridgman, P. W., *The Intelligent Individual and Society,* Macmillan, N. Y., 1938.

Dewey, J., *Reconstruction in Philosophy* (1920), Mentor, 1950.

*Frank, P., *Modern Science and its Philosophy,* Harvard University Press, 1949.

*Mises, R. von, *Positivism, a Study in Human Understanding,* Harvard University Press, 1951.

Pap, A., *Elements of Analytic Philosophy,* Macmillan, N. Y., 1949.

Pearson, K., *The Grammar of Science* (1892), Everyman's Library, N. Y., 1937.

Rapoport, A., *Operational Philosophy,* Harper and Bros., N. Y., 1954.

Reichenbach, H., *The Rise of Scientific Philosophy,* University of California Press, 1951.

Russell, B., *Human Society in Ethics and Politics,* Simon and Schuster, N. Y., 1955.

*Schlick, M., *Problems of Ethics,* Prentice-Hall, N. Y., 1939.

INDEX